Open Sesame

Open Sesame

Understanding American English and Culture
through Folktales and Stories

Planaria J. Price

Ann Arbor

THE UNIVERSITY OF MICHIGAN PRESS

Copyright © by the University of Michigan 1997
All rights reserved
ISBN 0-472-08388-0
Library of Congress Catalog Card No. 96-60157
Published in the United States of America by
The University of Michigan Press
Manufactured in the United States of America
Typeset by Codex Productions, Inc.

2000   1999   1998   1997   4   3   2   1

To my parents, Harold and Janet, who first told me these stories;
to Euphronia, who listened to my telling;
and to Murray, who waited while I wrote,
this book is dedicated with love.

Acknowledgments

I would like to thank the following people: Jim Goldstone, the first to believe; Kareen Kjelstrup, for introducing me to the University of Michigan Press; Mary Erwin, my editor, for giving me freedom and trust; Pam Hartmann—as always—for her advice and warm support; Ray Martin, my computer doctor, for making house calls; Ed Schwarz, my computer friend, for the shortcuts; Cliff Elmore, for erasing my writer's block; Xavier Urquieta, for his beautiful and sensitive illustrations; and, most of all, all my wonderful students at Evans Adult School, who showed me the magic of these stories.

Contents

A Parable

Once upon a time, in ancient Persia, there lived a man named Ali Baba. His father left him no inheritance and Ali Baba had married a poor woman. They struggled hard to put food on the table and clothes on their backs. But Ali Baba was a hard worker and a very observant man. One day he went to the forest to look for firewood. He heard a loud noise and saw a cloud of dust. Being curious, he hid behind a tree to see what he could see. Soon forty men rode by on horses. They stopped in front of a large rock. Each man then got off his horse and unloaded a large, heavy bag. The leader stood in front of the rock and in a loud voice said, "Open Sesame." At the sound of those words a door magically appeared in the rock, opened, and the forty men went inside with their forty bags. Ali Baba stayed behind the tree to see what he could see. A while later, the men came out and rode away.

Ali Baba came out from his hiding place, walked to the rock, faced it and in a loud voice said "Open Sesame." Just as before, at the sound of those words a door magically appeared in the rock and opened, and Ali Baba went in to see what he could see. He thought that he would find a dark and dangerous cavern, but instead he discovered a very beautiful room filled with bags and chests of gold and jewels.

From that day forward Ali Baba was a rich man. Whenever he needed more money, he would go to the rock and say "Open Sesame." He taught this magic to his children and they to their children, and they all lived happily ever after.

May this book be just as magical for you. Be as curious, hardworking, and observant as Ali Baba. Just say the words, "Open Sesame," and you will find, not a dark dangerous world of English, but a beautiful room full of the bright treasures of English and culture. These riches are for you to then bring home to your children and they to their children. And you will all live happily ever after.

Introduction to the Teacher and the Student

Why?

This book was written to help eliminate the terrible frustrations felt by both adult ESL students and their ESL teachers. Many students have studied English for years in their countries, in the United States, or in another English speaking country, but they still have difficulty understanding a simple conversation, catching the words of a television program, comprehending the meaning of a newspaper ad, and understanding American culture. Those students have many unanswered questions about vocabulary and American culture and feel extremely frustrated, fearing that they will struggle with English for a long, long time.

This frustration is often due to large gaps of knowledge of the basic, common "core" vocabulary and simple idioms of everyday English. Those common words are known to every native-speaking two year old. Yet those words are rarely learned by adult ESL students, who are taught only "adult vocabulary." Consequently adult ESL students often find themselves lost in common conversation and "simple" readings. Hand in hand with this problem is the fact that most ESL students were taught grammar rules first–almost in isolation from the natural language–with little chance to see how those rules really work in everyday, spoken English. Another problem is the great difficulty that nonnative speakers have in mastering the sounds, pronunciation, and intonations of English. Add to all these problems the fact that one cannot truly learn a language without also learning the culture. Not having been exposed to American culture, newcomers are often quite confused by both the extreme and the subtle differences between their native cultures and that of the United States. These differences cause embarrassment, misunderstanding, and lack of communication.

It is the purpose of this book to help bridge those gaps of vocabulary, idioms, and cultural awareness, easing the frustrations that students and their teachers experience.

How?

Following is an explanation of how this book will teach language and cultural fluency to foreign students.

Think about how all humans learn their native tongues. You would be surprised at the similarities in the nursery songs, lullabies, counting and singing games, rhymes, and stories found in all cultures. Although we adults think we

have forgotten them, those songs and stories remain deep within us, a funda-
mental part of us that helps to form our basic language patterns, our values, our
culture. The songs and stories that we heard as infants and children taught us
our language, its sounds and its rhythms. The stories taught us our grammar, the
structure of our language and its irregularities, as well as our core vocabulary and
idioms. And, as we grew older, the stories and songs taught us the values and
traditions of our culture.

By the age of five, we humans are fluent in our native language, and, at the
same time, as part of the same process by which we learned language, we have
absorbed the basic values of our cultures—our sense of right and wrong. In
adulthood, we remember neither learning language nor values but the early
experiences that led to this learning remain deep within us. Because of this,
references to the rhymes and stories of our childhood are used constantly and
unconsciously in everyday adult conversation in all cultures.

Thus, this book. Using it, you adult ESL students will successfully learn the
core vocabulary that you are missing, review concepts of basic grammar, reinforce
the sounds and intonations of the English language, and, most important of all,
learn the culture and values of the United States while having lively discussions
in which you compare and contrast the traditions and values of different native
cultures. The stories in this book are an important part of American literature,
and they are fun, and thought provoking. What you learn will remain with you,
increasing your fluency in American English and your understanding of American culture faster than more traditional approaches to learning English.

Part

How to Use This Book

Chapter  1

Being a Detective
to Solve the Puzzle of English

This book will be teaching you English and culture in the same way in which you learned your first language and culture when you were young. Children learn very quickly because they are natural detectives, using their eyes, ears, and brains to figure things out, finding different pieces of information, and fitting them slowly and patiently together like a puzzle. Children aren't afraid to experiment and have fun. We adults have lost that ability. We are afraid of making mistakes, we are in a hurry, we don't notice the small details, we have so much extra information from our personal experiences that we get confused. And, when we are learning something new, we are often afraid to experiment or have fun.

Well, it's impossible to become children again, but you can try to be a detective who has fun with the job. Open your eyes and look at the details in the stories and you will be surprised at how easy it will be to find clues to vocabulary and cultural values. *Pay close attention* to those details because just one small detail can help you guess the meaning of a word and show you the difference between one culture and another.

As you learn English you are constantly hearing and reading new words. The easiest and most comfortable thing to do is to immediately look up each new word in your dictionary, and translate the meaning so that you *understand* it. But are you *learning* English? Of course the answer is *no*! In an emergency situation, it is necessary to convey *information* immediately. But you are here to *learn* the language. Learning means struggling, questioning, repeating, forgetting, repeating again, making mistakes, and finally internalizing the sound of the word with the meaning. You cannot learn a language by translation. Translation gives you immediate information, and then you forget the word.

Think about how you learned your native language. When you were two years old and your mother said, "Don't touch the stove, it's hot," did you look up the word "hot" in a dictionary? Did your mother spell the word for you? Did she tell you if it was a noun or a verb, regular or irregular? Of course not. You touched the stove, burned your finger, and internalized, forever, the meaning of the word "hot." You learned your language by guessing the vocabulary by the context, the situation, by the words around the unfamiliar word.

Now look carefully at the following chapters of "puzzle pieces." These will help prepare you to solve the puzzles of vocabulary and culture in the stories in the book.

Chapter 2

Guessing Vocabulary from Context Clues

Here are some pieces to the puzzle of learning English. Look at the following types of context clues.

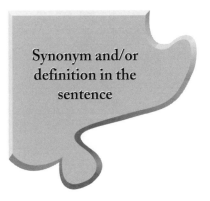

Synonym and/or definition in the sentence

1. *Definition:* Often a sentence will contain the definition of an unfamiliar word in the form of a synonym or the actual definition. For example, if you don't understand the word *context* read this sentence repeated from the next to last paragraph of chapter 1: "You learned your native language by guessing the vocabulary by the *context*, the situation, by the words around the unfamiliar word." If you look up the word *context* in a dictionary it will say *context: the situation, the surrounding words that help to explain the meaning.* But the dictionary wastes time and makes you lose your place and thought. If you simply read the sentence, you will *automatically* understand the

meaning of the word *context*. The definition is already there in front of your nose! Look at these examples.

a. Children learn their *native tongue*, their first language, from the stories and songs of their parents. The meaning of *native tongue* is ___my first language___ .

b. By the age of five, humans are *fluent* in their native language, understanding and being understood with ease. The meaning of *fluent* is ___understanding and being understood with ease___ .

c. It's easy, it's *a piece of cake!* The meaning of *a piece of cake* is ___it's so easy___ .

Antonym or contrast in the sentence

2. *Contrast*: Sometimes the unknown word is used in contrast to a word you do know, or it is explained by an antonym within the sentence. Contrasts are found less often because it is easier to find synonyms—or definitions—for *all* words, but an antonym must be *completely* opposite.

a. Ali Baba was a *pauper*, but when he found the treasures he became extremely rich. The meaning of *pauper* is _____.

b. Children have a hard time *coping* without their parents but can easily make decisions when their parents are with them. The meaning of *cope* is _____.

By example and by more details

3. *By Example and More Details:* Be sure to pay attention to each word in a sentence. Often there will be many details that will help you understand the basic meaning of the word even if you don't know the *exact* definition.
   a. Being *curious*, Ali Baba wanted to understand why the men were there, so he hid behind a tree to see what he could see. The meaning of *curious* is _____.
   b. Dorothy needed to find someone who could send her back to Kansas. Only a person with great magical powers could do that, so she went to find the *Wizard*. Dorothy needs a person of magic, and so she looks for a wizard. A *wizard* must be _____.

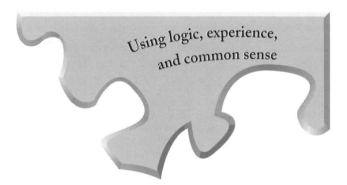

Using logic, experience, and common sense

4. *Logic and Experience:* One of the wonderful things about learning a language as an adult is that you know a lot about the world; your brain is filled with life experiences and adult logical thoughts. When you don't understand a word, look at the context and use your own common sense.
   a. The Little Red Hen wanted to make some bread so she put the flour, salt, water, and *yeast* into the bowl. You know that in order to make

bread you must have something that makes the bread rise up. It's not the flour, salt, or water. If you mixed those three together and baked them you would get a cracker. Therefore, *yeast* must mean _____ _____.

b. The third little pig built a *sturdy* little house of brick that the wolf could not blow down. If the house is made out of brick and if it can't be destroyed and it is called sturdy, then *sturdy* must mean _____.

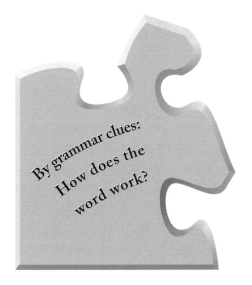

By grammar clues: How does the word work?

5. *Grammar Clues:* When you know the part of speech of a word, you can figure out a lot about it.

a. The shepherd and his son worked together *guarding* sheep against the wolves. *Guarding* is obviously a verb, an action. Ask yourself, what can one possibly do with sheep? You can play with a sheep, eat a sheep, shear a sheep (cut off its wool), or protect a sheep. When you look at the choices and add the information about the wolves, there is only one possibility. *To guard* is _____.

b. The baby bear spoke in a wee, tiny voice. You know that the words *wee* and *tiny* are adjectives. They are describing the voice of the baby bear. A voice can be big or little, loud or soft, friendly or angry. If a baby is speaking in that voice, *wee, tiny* must mean _____.

6. *Punctuation:* We use punctuation marks to help communicate meaning. Look at the dashes, commas, parentheses, and semicolons very carefully—they are there for a reason.

   a. Rapunzel had a thick blond braid—her hair was twisted together in three parts—and the witch could use it to climb up into the tower.

   b. Rapunzel had a thick blond braid, her hair was twisted together in three parts, and the witch could use it to climb up into the tower.

   c. Rapunzel had a thick blond braid (her hair was twisted together in three parts), and the witch could use it to climb up into the tower.

   The commas, dashes, and parentheses all convey the same information. A *braid* must mean _____.

   d. Hansel and Gretel's stepmother felt that the children were in the way during the famine—there was no food available.

   e. Hansel and Gretel's stepmother felt that the children were in the way during the famine, there was no food available.

   f. Hansel and Gretel's stepmother felt that the children were in the way during the famine (there was no food available).

   The dashes, commas, and parentheses all convey the same information. A *famine* must mean _____.

   Semicolon: A semicolon is used to join two strongly related ideas together. Often the phrase that follows the semicolon will add a clue to the unfamiliar word.

g. The tailors were very *wicked* men; they were dishonest and loved cheating people. So, *wicked* must mean _____.

h. The Scarecrow lacked *self-esteem;* he was insecure about his intelligence and didn't feel proud of his accomplishments. *Self-esteem* must mean

_____.

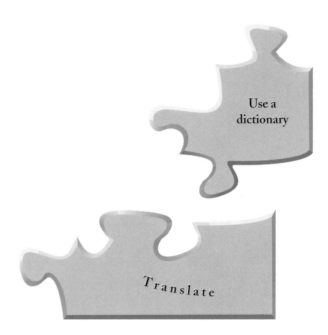

7. *Dictionary or Translation:* Of course you could always use a dictionary and/or translate the word, but then you would not be *learning* the language—you would merely understand what you read and then immediately forget the new vocabulary word. And, besides, translation is boring!

Answers:

2. a. a very poor person, the opposite of being extremely rich
    b. If you do not understand the word, you can figure out that it must be the opposite of *to make decisions easily.*

3. a. to want to understand things and to learn by observation
    b. a person with magical powers

4. a. that special substance that causes bread to be light and high
    b. strong

5. a. to protect
    b. very small

6. a, b, c. twisted together in three parts
    d, e, f. no food available
    g. someone who is dishonest and loves cheating people
    h. the quality of feeling good about yourself

Chapter  3

Solving the Puzzle of American Culture

Every culture has certain values and traditions that make it different from other cultures. These specific characteristics have developed as a result of the experiences of the people of that culture and the history of the people, and they change over time. Following is a brief description of "American" cultural characteristics. Please understand that these are extremely general statements describing the "average" American. As you look at the pieces of the puzzle of American culture, compare and contrast these values with the *average* values of your culture.

Because traditions develop from the past, in order to understand American culture, you need to know a *brief* history of the United States.

After the voyage of Christopher Columbus to the New World in 1492, England (like Spain, Portugal, France, and Holland) sent explorers to investigate and settle in this land. It was a time of exploration and scientific discoveries. When, in 1620, the English Puritans needed a place to live where they could have freedom of religion, they were able to come to the New World and start their own independent life. Their language was English, and their politics was English common law. They were serious, hardworking, deeply religious people. Because everyone had to be able to read the Bible, everyone received an education. American culture reflects some of the beliefs of these first people. Americans still believe in the importance of hard work and education and feel that having fun and doing "nothing" are a waste of time and somehow dangerous.

From 1620 to 1760, people came to the New World for freedom of choice. Thirteen different colonies were formed and each colony was extremely independent. The characteristics that those thirteen separate colonies did have in common were that their main language was English and that the people all valued hard work. The colonists believed that they deserved a better chance in life and that they had the free will to choose what they wanted. The land seemed endless and rich. If you were not happy or successful where you were, you could just move west and follow your dream.

When King George III of England started demanding tax money from the colonists, the thirteen different colonies sent representatives to meet together to discuss the situation. Those representatives were educated and open-minded. They believed that people make a government to serve the people and that when the government does not serve the people, it is the right of the people to change that government to help "the Safety and Happiness" of the people. In 1776 the colonists declared their independence from England by writing in a document "all men are created equal . . . . with certain unalienable Rights, that among these are Life, Liberty and the Pursuit of Happiness." This document is called the Declaration of Independence, and after it was written, the Revolutionary War— the War of Independence against England—began.

The Revolution was over in 1783. For six years there were still thirteen *independent* states, but the people soon realized that "in unity there is strength"; that separated they were weak. They knew that the thirteen separate governments must join together as one. To do this, they had to compromise. They decided to have a strong federal government but gave each state independence.

In 1788 the states approved the Constitution and elected George Washington to be the first president of the United States.

The country then grew quickly. The people (pioneers) moved westward to settle the enormous, rich, new land.

With this brief and simple history you may better understand the following "pieces to the puzzle" of why Americans think and act as they do.

1. Americans are extremely independent. They believe that to be truly free, they must have control over their own lives.

2. Because they want complete control over their lives, Americans value their privacy very much. "It's my life, it's my body, it's my room, it's my space."

3. Because Americans are independent, they must depend only on themselves. That is called self-reliance. They say, "No one tells me what to do. It's my life and my choice. I take the responsibility, and I must also pay the consequences. If I make a mistake, I have no one to blame but myself." Because of this individuality, American culture is not group centered like most cultures.

4. Americans are individuals and don't want to be the same as anyone else. They also believe that each individual is equal to all others. You are judged by who *you* are, not by your family, your job, the class you were born into, etc. Because of this belief, Americans feel that it is important to call people

by their personal names. Also, because Americans believe in treating every-one the same, their behavior in social situations is considered very informal.

5. Americans value hard work and distrust any kind of "laziness." In fact, they are a little afraid of unplanned "leisure," and they have to do something all the time. Even at a picnic, they rarely just sit around. There's always some-thing to do, some planned activity. Americans don't just stand around on the street; in fact, that's against the law in some situations!

6. Because of the value placed on hard work and their distrust of "class" Ameri-cans value the person who becomes successful by working from the bottom up on his or her own. Americans are not afraid to make mistakes or to admit that they made mistakes, because mistakes help you learn and improve.

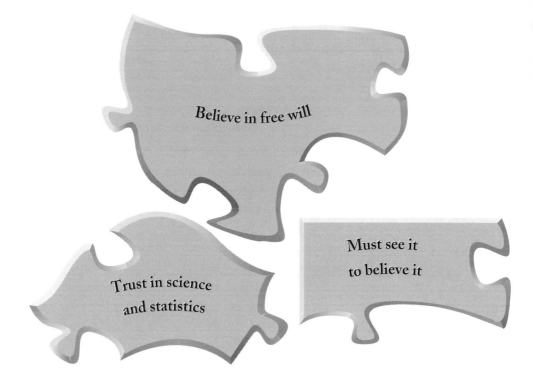

7. Because America developed during the Age of Science, Americans need to prove something before they believe it: "Prove it; show me; I have to see it with my own eyes." They trust science and feel very secure when they can explain things by facts and numbers (statistics). Because of this, they believe that there is a reason for everything, and they look for that reason. They do not believe in fate. They believe that they are the masters of their own destinies.

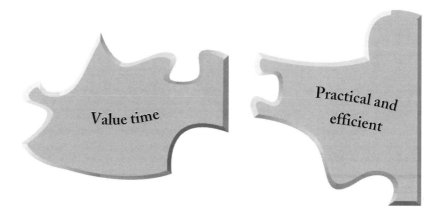

8. Americans are very practical. They look for the most efficient way to do something. They do not like to waste time, for after all, time is money.

Because of this, they are very direct and open in their speech: "Tell me what you want, don't talk around in circles."

9. Americans are extremely optimistic. They believe that human nature is basically good, and they plan for the future. They believe things can (and should) be "fixed," that bad things can be made better. Because of this, Americans will automatically offer advice on how to improve something (even if you don't ask for that advice!).

10. Americans are suspicious of a public show of *strong* emotions and value self-control. In contrast with many other cultures, Americans try to control their crying at funerals, avoid loud arguing or fighting in public, and rarely shout, whistle, etc. loudly in either anger or happiness in public.

11. Americans feel that the right to pursue happiness is the essential right of all human beings. They believe that each individual has a different definition of what happiness is and that each person has the right to try to find what will make him or her happy.

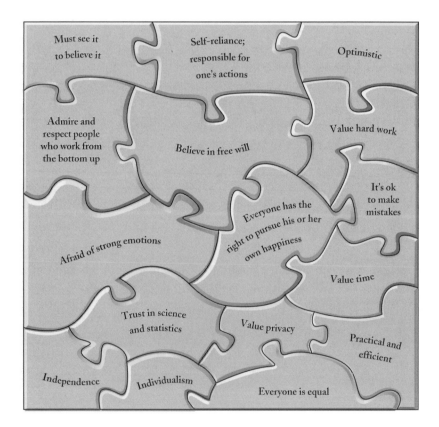

Chapter 4

Solving the Puzzle of Folktales, Fairy Tales, Hero Tales, and Tall Tales

This book contains twenty-six stories beloved by Americans. These stories hold an important place in the literature and culture of the United States. With the exception of one original story (chapter I of *Charlotte's Web)* all the stories have been retold by the author, but she has carefully retained the unique literary style of each story. Here are ten clues to help you understand how to learn cultural values from folktales.

1. In all cultures, stories told to children—folktales, fairy tales, hero tales, and tall tales—are an ancient method of transmitting a language and cultural values in an entertaining and enjoyable form. Most stories were originally oral, told over and over again by grandparents and parents to their children and handed down generation after generation. These stories often follow similar patterns in all cultures. They are very short. They seem very simple on the surface. There are not a lot of details. But, if you look carefully at *every* word, you will be surprised at the layers of meaning underneath. You

can enjoy the stories as a child does, looking only at the surface, literal meaning. Or you can enjoy the stories as an adult, looking deep at the cultural values being taught.

2.   These stories often help a child learn to grow and become an adult. They help children cope with their universal fears—the fear of the dark, fear of monsters, fear of the unknown, etc.

3.   The hero in the story is usually small. The hero could be a young child or a little animal or a small creature. A child hearing the story will, of course, identify with the small hero and learn the moral of the story in that way. The child will see the story through the eyes of the hero and understand the moral lesson through the hero's *point of view*.

4. Often the hero in the story is an orphan or lives with just one parent; the other parent has died or is away. This helps a child cope with the normal human fear of separation from one's parents.

5. The hero often lives in a safe place just on the edge of a dangerous place—a place that is dark or unknown. Depending on the culture (the geography of the country) the safe place could be on the edge of a forest, a jungle, a desert, an ocean, a river. It could be on the top of a mountain, under a volcano, etc. The choice of location is symbolic of how children feel. They are safe in their houses, but just outside they feel fear and danger.

6. The stories are usually about only *one* value. They teach only *one* lesson in a very *uncomplicated* way.

It just entertains

7. Sometimes the story has changed so much through time, that it has lost the original moral lesson. It just teaches the language, and, of course, it entertains.

Hero is "everyone"

8. Usually the hero has no name, or the name *describes* the hero. For example: Beauty, Snow White, the little pig. Sometimes the name describes what the hero does: the miller, the prince, the princess. Sometimes, when a real name is used, it is the most common first name of the culture: Jack, Gretel. Unless the story is a hero tale or legend, the hero is "everyone" and not a unique individual.

9. Often the hero must go on a journey. The journey symbolizes the *values* of the culture. If the hero obeys the values of the culture, he or she will survive. Those who do not follow the values will die or be terribly punished.

10. Usually the hero gets *three* chances to learn what is right. Often there are families of three brothers or three sisters. *Three* is a very important number in most folk tales from all countries.

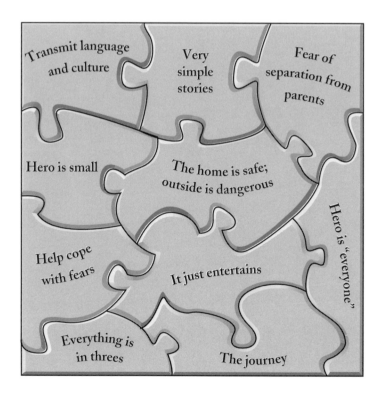

Part  2

Reading Selections

Chapter  5

You Can't Tell a Book by Its Cover

Beauty's but skin deep.
—John Davis of Hereford, 1585–1618

Things are seldom what they seem. Skim milk masquerades as cream.
—Sir William Gilbert, 1836–1911, *HMS Pinafore*

Cinderella

Reading Readiness

A. With a partner look at this advertisement. Describe what you see. Try to guess the names of the characters in the story and what the story will be about. Look at the sample description.

I see an advertisement for small shoes. I see the word fairy godmother (some kind of mother??) and I see a name, Cinderella — the same name as the title of the story. I think the story will be about small shoes, someone named Cinderella, and her mother.

Your Fairy Godmother Has Just Arrived!!

GRAND OPENING

Cinderella Shoes

Extra Small Sizes
2-5 AAAAAA-A

If the Shoe Doesn't Fit,
You Can't Wear It!

Palace Mall: Suite 153

B. Look at these questions and share your ideas with the class.

1. Have you ever been ignored by your family or friends? Did you feel they had all the fun and you had to do all the work? How did it make you feel?

2. Do you believe that goodness will be rewarded?

Background Notes

This story is about a young woman who is very good and patient but is mistreated by her stepmother and stepsisters. Fortunately, she meets a magical woman who protects her and helps her meet her Prince Charming.

This is the most common folktale found throughout the world. It has been told in Europe, in different versions, for over 1,000 years. The earliest story has been found in China, written in A.D. 850! Over 700 different versions have been collected. The American version comes from the story written in French by Charles Perrault in 1697 and translated into English in 1729. The story was made into an animated film by Walt Disney in 1950. You might want to watch the video after you read the story.

Reading Selection

Now read this story once, as quickly as possible, for the general idea. Try to guess the meanings of the words you don't understand by the context. You can underline the words you don't know, but don't stop reading. The first paragraph has been marked as an example.

Once upon a time there was a rich widower who had a daughter who was as beautiful as she was good. Soon after her mother died, her father married a widow who had two daughters. This woman was extremely conceited, as were her daughters. No sooner had they moved into the house, than they became very jealous of the beautiful young girl. They fired the servants and forced the young girl to clean and sweep and cook. The two stepsisters took over the girl's bedroom, which was filled with rich furniture, and her closet, which was filled with fine clothes. They made her sleep on the floor of the attic, and during the day she could only sit in the chimney corner among the cinders and weep. Because of this, they called her Cinderella. But Cinderella kept her sweetness and her beauty, which she had inherited from her mother.

One day the king's son decided to have a Ball. The three young girls were invited, but the wicked stepsisters would not let Cinderella go. "You have no clothes to wear, and your face is dirty," they said. But they made Cinderella help them prepare for the Ball. She had to sew their dresses and wash and iron. Then she had to fix their hair and choose their jewels. Any other girl would have stuck those nasty stepsisters with pins and tangled their hair, but not Cinderella.

Finally the day came and the stepsisters went off to the Ball. Cinderella went to her chimney corner and sobbed, "Oh, I wish I could, I wish I could, I wish I could go to the Ball." At that moment, her godmother, who was a fairy, appeared. "You wish to go to the Ball?" "Oh, fairy godmother, yes." "Then dry those tears and go outside and find me a large pumpkin." Cinderella brought a pumpkin to her godmother, who scooped out all of the seeds. Then with a touch of the fairy godmother's magic wand and an "Abracadabra" the pumpkin became a large coach covered in gold. "Now go to the mousetrap and bring me some mice." Cinderella found six live gray mice (the traps in those days were like cages so the lucky mice could keep their heads). Then with a touch of the magic wand and an "Abracadabra" the mice became six gray horses. "Now go find me a large rat." Cinderella went to the rattraps and brought back three rats. The fairy godmother chose the fattest one with the longest whiskers. Then with a touch of the magic wand and an "Abracadabra" the rat became a jolly coachman with a large beard. "Oh, fairy godmother how lovely, but I can't go to the Ball in these rags." With a touch of the fairy godmother's magic wand and an "Abracadabra" Cinderella was instantly clothed in a magnificent dress of gold and silver cloth, with the most beautiful glass slippers on her feet. "Now go to the Ball, my dear. But above all you must return before the clock strikes midnight, for the spell will not last a second longer."

Cinderella promised her godmother that she would return before midnight, and she went to the Ball. When the king's son saw her he was delighted by her beauty and asked her to dance. Everyone looked at her and wondered who this beautiful and rich princess was. She saw her stepsisters and smiled to them. Cinderella had a lovely time, but when she heard the clock strike eleven and three-quarters she said good-bye to the prince and hurried home. She immediately thanked her fairy godmother and asked if she could go again the next night, for the prince had invited her to return. When her sisters returned home they saw

Cinderella in the chimney corner and told her all about the beautiful and mysterious princess they had seen at the Ball.

The next day the two sisters returned to the Ball as did Cinderella. She had such a lovely time that she forgot about the spell. When she heard the clock strike twelve she ran as fast as she could. The prince ran after her, and a glass slipper fell off her foot and down the stair. The prince couldn't catch her, but he picked up the glass slipper and asked the palace guard if they had seen a beautiful princess running away. They said, "No, only a poor girl in rags."

The king's son told all the town that he would marry the girl whose foot could fit the glass slipper. They tried the shoe on all the royalty, but it didn't fit. Then they tried it on all the guests. When the king's minister came to the house of Cinderella, the sisters so badly wanted the slipper to fit that the elder took a knife and cut off her big toe, but the shoe was still too small. The younger took a knife and cut off her heel, but the shoe was still too small. Then Cinderella said, "Oh, let's see if it fits me." The sisters laughed, but the minister let her try on the slipper, and one, two, three, it fit perfectly. Then Cinderella took the other slipper out of her apron pocket and put it on. She was immediately taken to the palace, and the prince asked her to marry him even though she was still dressed in rags. Just then her fairy godmother arrived, and with a touch of her magic wand and an "Abracadabra" Cinderella was clothed in her magnificent dress of gold and silver cloth. They were soon married, and Cinderella and her Prince Charming lived happily ever after.

Checking Your Comprehension

Answer these questions in class.

1. Why are the stepsisters so mean to Cinderella?
2. Why is she called Cinderella?
3. The older French stories of Cinderella described her slippers as made of multicolored fur (*vair* in old French). Whether Perrault misheard the word as *verre* (glass) or he chose glass on purpose is not clear. Do you think it's important that the slipper be made of glass? Explain.

Be a Vocabulary Detective

Working in pairs, look for hints and guess the vocabulary from the context clues. Then fill in the blanks with the correct answers. Look at the example.

Clue 1

Poor Cinderella has to sleep in the *attic* under the roof and spend her days sitting in the chimney corner, where she gets very dirty in the *cinders*.

under the roof — she sleeps there — so it must be a room under the roof.

1. An *attic* is ___*a room at the top of a house for storage*___ (n).
   a) a basement   b) a bedroom   c) a room at the top of a house for storage

2. *Cinders* are_____(n)
   a) ashes   b) wood   c) sand

Clue 2

The stepmother is very *conceited* and thinks she is better and more beautiful than anyone else. She hates Cinderella, who *inherited* her sweetness and beauty from her mother. The stepmother married Cinderella's father, who is a *widower*.

3. *Conceited* means _____ (adj).
   a) humble   b) proud   c) sad

4. *inherit* means _____ (v).
   a) to receive   b) to steal   c) to love

5. A *widower* is_____(n).
   a) a father   b) a rich man   c) a man whose wife has died

Clue 3

Cinderella is helped by her *fairy godmother* who uses magic by waving a magic *wand* to make a magic *spell*. She helps Cinderella go to the prince's *Ball*, where she can dance until midnight. This wonderful woman can turn pumpkins into coaches by *scooping* out the seeds and turn rats with long *whiskers* into coachmen with large beards.

6. A *fairy godmother* is _____ (n).
   a) a grandmother b) mother's best friend c) a magical caretaker

7. A *wand* is _____ (n).
   a) a magical stick b) money c) a hand

8. A *spell* is _____(n).
   a) forming words correctly b) a magical change c) leaking water

9. A *Ball* is _____(n).
   a) a round toy b) a fancy dance c) a dinner party

10. *Scoop* means _____ (v).
    a) to fill b) to empty c) to fly

11. *Whiskers* are _____ (n).
    a) hair on the face b) hair on the arms c) hair on the head

Clue 4

Cinderella is so sweet that she carefully combs the hair of her sisters until it is smooth and beautiful and she doesn't *tangle* it.

12. *Tangle* means _____(v).
    a) to make messy b) to separate c) to shine

Questions for Discussion

First, reread the story carefully looking for the deeper meanings and reviewing the vocabulary. Then in groups of four discuss the following questions with your classmates. Be sure to tell what your native culture is. An example has been given to the first question.

1. What was your favorite sentence in this story and why?

My favorite sentence was when Cinderella helped dress her stepsisters and it said "Any other girl would have stuck those nasty stepsisters with pins and tangled their hair, but not Cinderella." I certainly wouldn't have helped those nasty girls. I would have stuck them with pins!!!

2. Do you think Cinderella deserved to have such a happy ending?

3. Should the stepmother and stepsisters receive more punishment or should they be forgiven?

Putting All the Pieces Together

Look at the puzzles on page 18 and page 23. Find the pieces that fit this story and discuss what cultural values this folktale teaches American children.

Double-checking the Vocabulary

Match the definitions with the words.

a. hair coming out of the face
b. a condition caused by magical power
c. to remove something with an upward motion
d. a thin stick that causes magic to happen
e. a man whose wife has died
f. having a high opinion of oneself
g. a fancy dance
h. ashes from a fire
i. a room just below the roof
j. a magical person who protects
k. to cause to become confused and twisted
l. to receive a characteristic, property, or money from someone else—in the case of property or money, usually after the giver's death

1. widower
2. conceited
3. attic
4. cinders
5. Ball
6. inherit
7. tangle
8. wand
9. fairy godmother
10. scoop
11. whiskers
12. spell

Writing

Think, *in English*, about the most similar story in your culture. Then, using the vocabulary words, write it, *in English*, in correct American form and as briefly as possible. The story written here is a good example of a similar story from a different culture.

The Chinese Cinderella

When I was very little in Hainan, China, my grandmother told me the story of Yeh-Hsien. She was not conceited but a very nice little girl and very lovely. She had no mother or father but had a very mean stepmother, who was a widow. Her only friends were the catfish with whiskers she talked to in the lake near her house. The mean stepmother <u>scooped</u> the fish out of the lake and killed them. But a man came down from the sky and told Yeh-Hsien that the bones of the fish would make her wishes come true. He was like a <u>fairy godfather</u>! She wished for fine clothes and golden slippers to go to a <u>Ball</u> in the town. As she danced she lost one of her shoes and a beggar found it and sold it to the king who was amazed by the small size of the shoe. He found Yeh-Hsien and they got married and her mean stepmother was killed by a magic <u>spell</u> that made rocks fall from the sky.

When I was little, I always made wishes over fish bones. It was always the same wish, to come to America, and look!! my wish came true like Yeh-Hsien's.

Speaking

Now, tell your story.

The Princess and the Pea

Reading Readiness

A. With a partner look at this advertisement. Describe what you see. Try to guess the names of the characters in the story and what the story will be about.

B. Look at these questions and share your ideas with the class.

1. Have you ever tossed and turned all night because there was something sticking you in the bed? Describe how it felt.

2. Can you tell if someone is a good person just by looking at him or her? Explain your answer.

No More Tossing and Turning When You Cover Your Old Lumpy Mattress with Princess Foam Mattress Pad. Whether You Have Rocks or Peas in Your Old Mattress, Princess Egg Crate Style Mattress Pads Will Shield Even the Most Tender of Skins.

Available Where All Quality Bedding Is Sold.

Or Call 1-800-PRINCESS

Background Notes

This is a story about a young prince who, when looking for a wife, is not satisfied with any young women he meets. Then he meets a woman who claims to be a real princess, but his mother wants to be sure. This story was told to Hans Christian Andersen when he was a little boy in Denmark. He wrote it down in 1835 in a book of children's stories. The book and Andersen immediately became famous throughout the world. This story was translated into English in 1846. The theme is common throughout the world—that princesses (and actresses, sports stars, musicians, etc.) are different from the rest of us.

Reading Selection

Now read this story once, as quickly as possible, for the general idea. Try to guess the meanings of the words you don't understand by the context. You can underline the words you don't know, but don't stop reading.

Once upon a time, there lived a prince, and he wanted to marry a princess, but she must be a *real* princess. He traveled all around the world to find one, but there was always something wrong with the maidens. He found plenty of princesses, but he never could find out if they were *real* princesses, for sometimes one thing and sometimes another thing about the ladies just didn't seem right. At last he returned home quite dejected, for he wanted so very much to have a real princess for a wife.

One evening, there was a terrible storm. There was thunder, there was lightning, and it was raining cats and dogs. There was not a star to be seen in the sky, and it was extremely dark. Suddenly there was a loud knocking on the castle door. The old king went out himself to see who was there.

There was a young girl standing at the door, and oh my heavens! what a mess she was from the rain! The water ran down from her hair, and her dress was sopping wet and stuck to her body. She looked terrible, but she said she was a real princess.

"We'll soon see," thought the old queen. She did not say a word but went into the guest bedroom and took all the bedding off the bed and laid a small green pea on the bottom of the bed frame. Then she took twenty mattresses and laid them one upon the other on the pea. When that was done, she took twenty feather beds and put these on top of the mattresses.

This was the bed the princess was to sleep in. She had to climb onto it with a ladder!

The next morning the queen asked the princess if she had slept well.

"Oh, no! I don't want to sound ungrateful, dear Queen, but I had a horrid night!" said the princess. "I was hardly able to close my eyes the whole night! Heaven knows what was in my bed, but there was something hard under me, and my whole body is black and blue with bruises! I can't tell you what I've suffered!"

Then they knew that the lady was a *real* princess because she had felt the small pea through twenty mattresses and twenty feather beds. It was quite impossible for anyone but a true princess to be so tender.

So the prince married her, for he was now convinced that he had a real princess for his wife, and they lived happily ever after.

And the pea was put in the museum, where it still can be seen, if no one has stolen it.

Checking Your Comprehension

Answer these questions in class.

1. Why does it take so long for the prince to find a wife?
2. Why does the princess look so bad when she knocks on the door?
3. Why does the queen put twenty mattresses and twenty feather beds on the princess's bed frame?

Be a Vocabulary Detective

Working in pairs, look for hints and guess the vocabulary from the context clues. Then fill in the blanks with the correct answers.

Clue 1

The prince travels all around the world to find a young princess but cannot find one. He returns home *dejected* because he met many *maidens* but not one pleased him.

1. To be *dejected* means to feel _____(adj).
   a) sad   b) happy   c) pretty

2. A *maiden* is _____ (n).
   a) a little girl   b) an unmarried woman   c) an old woman

Clue 2

There is a terrible rainstorm, and it is *raining cats and dogs*. The princess is walking in the rain, and she is *sopping wet*. Because her clothes are all wet, she looks like a *mess*.

3. *To rain cats and dogs* means _____ (idiom).
   a) to love animals   b) to rain hard   c) to make noise

4. To be *sopping wet* means _____ (adj).
   a) to be dry   b) to be cold   c) to be extremely wet

5. To be a *mess* means _____ (n).
   a) to be organized   b) to be disorganized c) to be poor

Clue 3

The queen knows that only real princesses are extremely sensitive. The princess can't sleep all night and says it was a *horrid* night. Because she has very *tender* skin the poor princess has *bruises* on her body and feels all *black and blue* because of the pea.

6. *Horrid* means _____ (adj).
   a) terrible   b) wonderful   c) frightening

7. *Tender* means _____ (adj).
   a) hard   b) soft   c) sick

8. A *bruise* is _____ (n).
   a) a sore   b) a bump   c) a scar

9. To be *black and blue* means _____ (idiom).
   a) to be colorful   b) to have tattoos   c) to feel sore

Clue 4

The queen tries to hide the pea by putting twenty *feather beds* and twenty mattresses on the bed frame.

10. A *feather bed* is _____ (n).
    a) a mattress filled with water
    b) a mattress filled with cotton
    c) a mattress filled with the hair of chickens, duck, or geese

Clue 5

The princess is very thankful that they let her sleep in the palace, but she must tell the truth even though she will sound *ungrateful*.

11. To be *ungrateful* means _____ (adj).
    a) to be thankful   b) to be sincere   c) to be unthankful

Questions for Discussion

First, reread the story carefully looking for the deeper meanings and reviewing the vocabulary. Then in groups of four discuss the following questions with your classmates. Be sure to tell what your native culture is.

1. What was your favorite sentence in this story and why?
2. Do you think people today still think that "royalty" are different than ordinary people? You can use examples of a princess of England or a famous sports star or movie star.
3. Do you think that the prince loved the princess for who she *really* was? Does anybody love anybody else for who he or she really is?

Putting All the Pieces Together

Look at the puzzles on page 18 and page 23. Find the pieces that fit this story and discuss what cultural values this folktale teaches American children.

Double-checking the Vocabulary

Look at the definitions and cross out the words in the list that match. Then, looking at the words that remain, read from left to right, top to bottom, and find the answer to the question, "What did the prince say to the princess?"

a. extremely and thoroughly wet
b. a young unmarried woman
c. a large heavy cloth filled with feathers; it is soft and keeps you very warm
d. feeling very sad and disappointed
e. an idiom to describe a heavy rain
f. extremely soft and sensitive
g. not showing any thanks
h. terrible
i. an idiom to describe the mark on the skin from being hit (the blood stays under the skin)
j. where the skin has been injured but not broken
k. extreme disorder
l. small round vegetables

maiden	oh!	dejected	to rain cats and dogs
mess	sopping wet	please	horrid
marry	ungrateful	peas	black and blue
bruise	tender	me	feather bed

Writing

Think, *in English*, about the most similar story in your culture. Then, using the vocabulary words, write it, *in English*, in correct American form and as briefly as possible.

Speaking

Now, tell your story.

The Ugly Duckling

Reading Readiness

A. With a partner look at this advertisement. Describe what you see. Try to guess the names of the characters in the story and what the story will be about.

B. Look at these questions and share your ideas with the class.

1. Do you remember when you were a teenager? Your arms and legs were growing fast; your skin had pimples; you felt very unsure. Did you feel that you were ugly or beautiful? Did you feel that you fit in with everyone else? Describe how you felt.

2. Have you ever wanted to trade places with someone else? Why? Who?

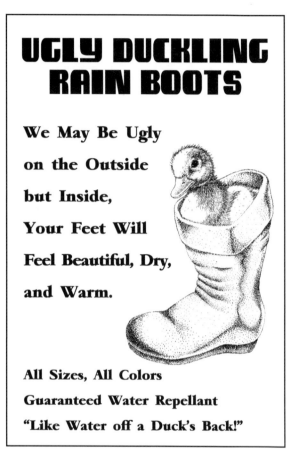

UGLY DUCKLING RAIN BOOTS

We May Be Ugly on the Outside but Inside, Your Feet Will Feel Beautiful, Dry, and Warm.

All Sizes, All Colors
Guaranteed Water Repellant
"Like Water off a Duck's Back!"

Background Notes

This story about a young duck who looks so different from his brothers and sisters that he runs away from home was written by Hans Christian Andersen of Denmark in 1845. Many people think that it is his "autobiography" because Andersen always felt he was a failure and no one recognized his talents until he was old. You might want to watch a video of the 1952 musical with Danny Kaye called *Hans Christian Andersen*. It's the story of his life.

Reading Selection

Now read this story once, as quickly as possible, for the general idea. Try to guess the meanings of the words you don't understand by the context. You can underline the words you don't know, but don't stop reading.

Once upon a time, a long time ago, a mother duck was sitting on her eggs. The eggs began to hatch. "Peep, peep, peep," said the baby ducks. "Quack, quack, quack," said the proud mother, ready to lead them to the river for their first swim. But there was still one egg left. The mother was patient, like all mothers are, and finally the egg hatched; but out came the ugliest duckling she had ever seen! He tripped on his big feet when he walked, and he was so clumsy that he kept falling on his face. When they got to the river, however, he swam just beautifully, and she felt proud of her ugly son. But the other animals on the farm made fun of him, mocked him, and pecked him. His brothers and sisters laughed at him and said they hoped the cat would eat him. As time passed, even his mother grew ashamed that he was hers. So the ugly duckling ran away to the deep woods.

Even in the forest all the animals laughed at him—the wild ducks, geese, and rabbits. So he lived alone on the forest lake all summer. When the autumn came, it began to get very cold. One day he saw some beautiful, graceful white birds flying overhead to the warmer southern lands. Oh, how he wished he could be as beautiful as those strange birds. When winter came, he was so cold and lonely that he cried himself to sleep each night. One night the water got so cold it froze, and he got stuck in the lake. He knew he was going to die.

The next morning a farmer saw the frozen duck, freed him from the ice, and brought him home to his wife and children. The children wanted to play with the duckling, but he was too afraid of them. He flapped his wings in a bowl of milk, and flew in and out of the flour bin. When the woman screamed at the mess, he ran away to the woods where he spent a very sad winter all alone.

At last spring came, and the days started to get warmer. One day he heard a whirr of wings above his head and saw those same magnificent white birds he had seen flying south in the autumn. They landed on his lake. "I will go over to those royal birds and they will peck me to death because I am so ugly, but better to be killed by these magnificent creatures than pecked at by ordinary ducks and chickens." So he swam over to those white birds, and they ruffled their feathers. He bowed his head awaiting death and saw his reflection in the clear stream. But the reflection was no longer an ugly and clumsy gray bird. It was a beautiful white swan! The other swans swam around him and stroked him with their beaks. Little children on the shore said, "Look, there's a new swan and it's the prettiest, so young and handsome!" and they threw bread into the water.

He felt quite shy and hid his head under his wing. He did not know what to think. He was bursting with happiness, but he was not feeling conceited. A good heart never becomes conceited. He thought, "I never dreamed of such happiness when I was an ugly duckling. It doesn't matter about being born in a duck yard as long as you are hatched from a swan's egg."

Checking Your Comprehension

Answer these questions in class.
1. Why does the ugly duckling look so different from his brothers and sisters?
2. Why does everyone mock him?
3. Why does he burst with happiness at the end of the story?

Be a Vocabulary Detective

Working in pairs, look for hints and guess the vocabulary from the context clues. Then fill in the blanks with the correct answers.

Clue 1

The mother duck has to sit on the eggs and wait for the eggs to *hatch*. Although it takes a long time, she is very *patient*.

1. *Hatch* means _____ (v).
    a) to open   b) to close   c) to die

2. *Patient* means _____ (adj).
    a) able to wait   b) unable to wait   c) kind

Clue 2

The farm animals, and even his brothers and sisters, are very mean to the ugly duckling. They laugh at him and *mock* him. The ducks and chickens *peck* him and attack him with their *beaks*.

3. *Mock* means _____ (v).
    a) to eat   b) to love   c) to make fun of

4. *Peck* means _____ (v).
   a) to kiss   b) to bite   c) to look

5. A *beak* is _____ (n).
   a) the mouth of a bird   b) an egg   c) a rock

Clue 3

The ugly duckling hears a *whirr*. He looks into the sky and sees beautiful swans *flapping* their wings as they fly in the air overhead. When the swans land on the lake they *ruffle* their feathers and swim over to the ugly duckling and *stroke* his feathers with their beaks.

6. A *whirr* is _____ (n).
   a) a sound of movement   b) an airplane   c) a bird

7. *Flap* means _____(v).
   a) to make noise   b) to move quickly   c) to fall down

8. *Ruffle* means _____ (v).
   a) to make even   b) to make uneven   c) to hit

9. *Stroke* means _____ (v).
   a) to bite   b) to rub   c) to knock

Clue 4

The ugly duckling can't walk or fly as easily as his brothers or sisters because he is very *clumsy*. He thinks that the wild swans are very *graceful*.

9. *Clumsy* means _____ (adj).
   a) elegant   b) awkward   c) fat

10. *Graceful* means _____(adj).
    a) beautiful   b) ugly   c) able to move easily

Clue 5

When winter comes, the lake gets so cold it *freezes* and the ugly duckling gets stuck in the ice.

11. *Freeze* means _____ (v).
    a) to turn to ice   b) to turn to water   c) to become gas

Questions for Discussion

First, reread the story carefully looking for the deeper meanings and reviewing the vocabulary. Then in groups of four discuss the following questions with your classmates. Be sure to tell what your native culture is.

1. What was your favorite sentence in this story and why?
2. Does the way a person sees himself or herself determine his or her success or failure?
3. Why do humans make fun of people who look different?

Putting All the Pieces Together

Look at the puzzles on page 18 and page 23. Find the pieces that fit this story and discuss what cultural values this folktale teaches American children.

Double-checking the Vocabulary

Fill in the crossword with the following vocabulary words: stroke, beak, patient, froze, peck, hatch, flap, ruffle, whirr, mock, clumsy, graceful.

Across

1. to move something up and down, making a noise
2. to make a soft repetitive sound, like something beating in the air
3. able to wait calmly
4. when liquid turned to solid because of a low temperature
5. fineness and ease in movement
6. to make fun of

Down

3. to strike with a beak
7. to cause to break or open so something can come out
8. to make uneven
9. the hard mouth of a bird; also called a bill
10. to touch or rub softly
11. awkward and ungraceful

Writing

Think, *in English*, about the most similar story in your culture. Then, using the vocabulary words, write it, *in English*, in correct American form and as briefly as possible.

Speaking

Now, tell your story.

Chicken Little

Reading Readiness

A. With a partner look at this political cartoon. Describe what you see. Try to guess the names of the characters in the story and what the story will be about.

The Sky Is Falling!

B. Look at these questions and share your ideas with the class.
1. Have you ever believed a rumor and then found out later it wasn't true?
2. How do you know when to believe something and when to question it?

Background Notes

This story about some farmyard animals who hear a rumor that something terrible is happening and go to warn the king is from an old English nursery tale first called "Chicken Licken" and made popular as "Henny Penny" in 1892 in the book *English Fairy Tales* by Joseph Jacobs. It is usually told as "Chicken Little" in the United States. Very young children love this story because of the sounds: the silly rhyming names, predictable repetition, and additions. They beg to hear it over and over again.

Reading Selection

Now read this story once, as quickly as possible, for the general idea. Try to guess the meanings of the words you don't understand by the context. You can underline the words you don't know, but don't stop reading.

One bright day Chicken Little was digging for seeds under an oak tree in the barnyard when "whack," a hard acorn hit her on the head. "Goodness, gracious me!" said Chicken Little. "The sky is falling. The sky is falling. I must go and tell the king."

So she went along and went along, and soon she met Cocky-Locky. "Where are you going, Chicken Little?" said Cocky-Locky. "Oh, the sky is falling and I must go and tell the king." "May I come with you?" said Cocky-Locky. "Certainly," said Chicken Little. So Chicken Little and Cocky-Locky went to tell the king the sky was falling.

They went along and went along, and soon they met Ducky-Waddles. "Where are you going, Chicken Little and Cocky-Locky?" said Ducky-Waddles. "Oh, the sky is falling and we must go and tell the king." "May I come with you?" said Ducky-Waddles. "Certainly," said Chicken Little and Cocky-Locky.

So Chicken Little, Cocky-Locky, and Ducky-Waddles went to tell the king the sky was falling.

They went along and went along, and soon they met Goosey-Loosey. "Where are you going, Chicken Little, Cocky-Locky, and Ducky-Waddles?" "Oh, the sky is falling and we must go and tell the king." "May I come with you?" said Goosey-Loosey. "Certainly," said Chicken Little, Cocky-Locky, and Ducky-Waddles. So Chicken Little, Cocky-Locky, Ducky-Waddles, and Goosey-Loosey went to tell the king the sky was falling.

They went along and went along, and soon they met Turkey-Lurkey. "Where are you going, Chicken Little, Cocky-Locky, Ducky-Waddles, and Goosey-Loosey?" "Oh, the sky is falling and we must go and tell the king." "May I come with you?" said Turkey-Lurkey. "Certainly," said Chicken Little, Cocky-Locky, Ducky-Waddles, and Goosey-Loosey.

So Chicken Little, Cocky-Locky, Ducky-Waddles, Goosey-Loosey, and Turkey-Lurkey went to tell the king the sky was falling.

They went along and went along until they met Foxy-Woxy. "Where are you going, Chicken Little, Cocky-Locky, Ducky-Waddles, Goosey-Loosey, and Turkey-Lurkey?"

"Oh, the sky is falling and we must go and tell the king."

"Oh, but this is not the way to the king. I know the proper way. Shall I show you?" said Foxy-Woxy. "Certainly." said Chicken Little, Cocky-Locky, Ducky-Waddles, Goosey-Loosey, and Turkey-Lurkey. So Chicken Little, Cocky-Locky, Ducky-Waddles, Goosey-Loosey, Turkey-Lurkey, and Foxy-Woxy all went to tell the king the sky was falling.

So they went along and went along, until they came to a narrow and dark hole. Now this was the door to Foxy-Woxy's cave. But Foxy-Woxy said to Chicken Little, Cocky-Locky, Ducky-Waddles, Goosey-Loosey, and Turkey-Lurkey, "This is the shortcut to the king's palace. You'll get there faster if you follow me. I will go first and you come after." "Why of course, certainly, without doubt, why not?" said Chicken Little, Cocky-Locky, Ducky-Waddles, Goosey-Loosey, and Turkey-Lurkey.

So Foxy-Woxy went into his cave, and he didn't go very far but turned around to wait for Chicken Little, Cocky-Locky, Ducky-Waddles, Goosey-Loosey, and Turkey-Lurkey.

First Turkey-Lurkey went through the dark hole into the cave. He hadn't gone far when "crunch!" Foxy-Woxy snapped off Turkey-Lurkey's head. Then Goosey-Loosey went in and "crunch!" off went her head, and Goosey-Loosey was thrown in a heap beside Turkey-Lurkey. Then Ducky-Waddles waddled down, and her head was soon snapped off. Then Cocky-Locky strutted down into the cave, and he hadn't gone far when "snap, crunch!" went Foxy-Woxy, and Cocky-Locky was thrown alongside of Goosey-Loosey, Turkey-Lurkey, and Ducky-Waddles. But Foxy-Woxy had to make two bites at Cocky-Locky. The first snap only hurt Cocky-Locky, and he screamed out to Chicken Little. She turned tail and off she ran home, so she never got to tell the king that the sky was falling.

_____

Checking Your Comprehension

Answer these questions in class.
1. Why does Chicken Little think that the sky is falling?
2. Where are the animals going?

3. Where does Foxy-Woxy lead them?
4. How does Chicken Little escape?

Be a Vocabulary Detective

Working in pairs, look for hints and guess the vocabulary from the context clues. Then fill in the blanks with the correct answers.

Clue 1

All the animals believe the *rumor* that the sky is falling.

1. A *rumor* is _____ (n).
   a) a true story   b) an unproven story   c) a lie

Clue 2

An *acorn* falls from an oak tree and *whacks* Chicken Little on the head.

2. An *acorn* is _____ (n).
   a) a flower   b) a leaf   c) a hard seed

3. *Whack* means _____ (v).
   a) to kiss   b) to hit   c) to touch

Clue 3

Foxy-Woxy says he knows a *shortcut* to the king's palace so the animals can get there quickly. The animals believe Foxy-Woxy and don't *doubt* him. But Foxy-Woxy takes them to his *cave* instead.

4. A *shortcut* is _____ (idiom).
   a) a slow way   b) a fast way   c) a freeway

5. *Doubt* means _____ (v).
   a) to know   b) to believe   c) to question

6. A *cave* is _____ (n).
   a) a house   b) a cage   c) a hole in a rock

Clue 4

Ducky-Waddles is a duck and Cocky-Locky is a rooster, and they walk in different ways. The duck *waddles*. The cock *struts*.

7. *Waddle* means_____ (v).
   a) to walk from side to side   b) to run   c) to swim

8. A *cock* is _____ (n).
   a) a male chicken   b) a swan   c) an alcoholic drink

9. *Strut* means _____ (v).
   a) to walk proudly   b) to fly   c) to crawl

Clue 5

Foxy-Woxy bites off the animals' heads with a *"crunch."* Then he throws all the dead birds in a *heap* except for Chicken Little, who is lucky to *turn tail* and run home.

10. *Crunch* means_____ (n).
    a) a quiet sound   b) a noisy sound   c) a swallow

11. A *heap* is _____ (n).
    a) a pile   b) an empty place   c) a closet

12. *Turn tail* means _____ (v).
    a) to come together   b) to turn in circles   c) to run away quickly

Questions for Discussion

First, reread the story carefully looking for the deeper meanings and reviewing the vocabulary. Then in groups of four discuss the following questions with your classmates. Be sure to tell what your native culture is.

1. What was your favorite sentence in this story and why?
2. Do you think the animals deserved the punishment they received?
3. Do you think it was fair that Chicken Little got to escape?

Putting All the Pieces Together

Look at the puzzles on page 18 and page 23. Find the pieces that fit this story and discuss what cultural values this folktale teaches American children.

Double-checking the Vocabulary

Look at the definitions and cross out the words in the list that match. Then, looking at the words that remain, read from left to right, top to bottom, and find the answer to the question, "What did Chicken Little think?"

a. to walk with short steps bending from side to side because the body is heavy and the legs short
b. a natural, deep, hollow place in a rock or under ground
c. to go the opposite way quickly
d. unofficial news, common talk, probably not true
e. a mass of things one on top of the other
f. the nut of the oak tree
g. to walk in a proud, strong way
h. to hit with a blow making a loud noise
i. to be unsure
j. the fastest way to a place
k. to crush food noisily with the teeth
l. the "husband" of the chicken

rumor	whack	the	acorn
waddle	sky	shortcut	doubt
heap	strut	is	turn tail
falling	crunch	cock	cave

Writing

Think, *in English*, about the most similar story in your culture. Then, using the vocabulary words, write it, *in English*, in correct American form and as briefly as possible.

Speaking

Now, tell your story.

Little Red Riding Hood

Reading Readiness

A. With a partner look at this advertisement. Describe what you see. Try to guess the names of the characters in the story and what the story will be about.

B. Look at the questions and share your ideas with the class.
   1. In this story the old grandmother lives all alone and far away from the family. Is that common in your culture?
   2. What lessons would a mother in your culture teach her child before the child goes for a walk in the woods?

Background Notes

In this fairy tale from France, written by Charles Perrault in 1697, a little girl, who wears a red hat, brings food to her sick grandmother. She has to walk through a forest and meets a wolf. The story was first published in English in 1729. It was collected by the German brothers Jacob and Wilhelm Grimm (the Brothers Grimm) who changed the sad but more realistic ending to make it happy.

Reading Selection

Now read this story once, as quickly as possible, for the general idea. Try to guess the meanings of the words you don't understand by the context. You can underline the words you don't know, but don't stop reading.

There was once upon a time a little village girl, the prettiest ever seen or known. Her mother loved her very much, but her grandmother loved her even more and made a little red coat with a cap for the child. This hood was so perfect that wherever she went she was known by the name of Little Red Riding Hood.

One day, her mother baked some cakes and said to her, "Go and see how your grandmother is feeling, for I have been told she is ill. Take this cake and this little bottle of wine to her. Go quickly before the weather gets hot. Don't loiter by the way and don't talk to any strangers." So Little Red Riding Hood started off without delay toward the village in which her grandmother lived. On her way she had to pass through a wood where she met a wolf. She was quite naive and did not know what a wicked animal he was, so she was not a bit afraid of him.

"Good morning, Little Red Riding Hood." he said.

"Good morning," said Little Red Riding Hood.

"Where are you going and what is in your basket?" asked the wolf.

"I'm bringing cake and wine to my grandmother. She is sick, and it will make her well."

"Where does your grandmother live, Little Red Riding Hood?"

"On the further side of the mill that you see down there; hers is the first house in the village."

The wolf walked along with Little Red Riding Hood awhile. Then he said, "Look at the pretty flowers. Why don't you look about you? You are so solemn. Everything else here is so happy."

Little Red Riding Hood raised her eyes, and when she saw the bright flowers she thought, "I'm sure grandmother would be pleased if I took her a bunch of fresh flowers. It is still early. I shall have plenty of time to pick them."

In the meantime the wolf ran as fast as he could to Grandmother's house. He knocked on the door, "tap, tap, tap."

"Who is there?"

"It is your granddaughter, Little Red Riding Hood," answered the wolf, imitating a child's voice. "I have brought a cake and a bottle of wine from my mother."

The good grandmother, who was ill in bed, called out, "Pull up the latch." The wolf did, and the door opened. He leaped on the poor old woman and gobbled her up in no time, for he hadn't eaten for three days. He then shut the door, put on her nightgown and nightcap, and got into bed.

Soon Little Red Riding Hood came and knocked at the door, "tap, tap, tap." "Who is there?" Little Red Riding Hood was frightened on hearing the wolf's gruff voice, but, thinking her grandmother had a cold, she answered. "It is your granddaughter, Little Red Riding Hood. I have brought a cake and a bottle of wine from my mother."

The wolf called out, "Pull up the latch." The door opened, and Little Red Riding Hood went in. "Put the cake and the wine in the cupboard and come into bed with me." Little Red Riding Hood was surprised to see how different her grandmother looked lying in bed. "Grandmother, what long arms you have!"

"All the better to hug you with, my dear."

"Grandmother, what long legs you have!"

"All the better to run with, my sweet."

"Grandmother, what long ears you have!"

"All the better to hear you with, my dear."

"Grandmother, what large eyes you have!"

"All the better to see you with, my sweet."

"Grandmother, what large teeth you have!"

"All the better to eat you with, my dear."

And saying these words, the wicked wolf sprang on Little Red Riding Hood and ate her up.

Now that's the original story. Most children are too ignorant of the real meaning of death to be hurt by this ending. Children have logical minds, and this is a logical conclusion. It teaches a strong lesson. But many modern adults, seeing the story through adult eyes, prefer the happier ending of the Grimm tale, which follows.

After the wolf ate Little Red Riding Hood, he fell into a deep sleep and was soon snoring loudly. A huntsman went past the cottage and thought, "How loudly the old lady is snoring! I must see if anything is the matter with her." When he went in, he saw the wolf and took a knife and cut open the wolf's stomach. Out sprang the little girl and her grandmother. Then the huntsman gathered some stones, filled the wolf's stomach, and sewed him closed. When the wolf woke up he tried to spring out of bed, but the stones dragged him back and he fell down dead.

Little Red Riding Hood thought to herself, "I will never again wander off into the forest when my mother forbids it."

Checking Your Comprehension

Answer these questions in class.
1. List three things Little Red Riding Hood's mother tells her.
2. Does Little Red Riding Hood follow her mother's advice?
3. Where does the grandmother live? Why?

Be a Vocabulary Detective

Working in pairs, look for hints and guess the vocabulary from the context clues. Then fill in the blanks with the correct answers.

Clue 1

Little Red Riding *Hood* looks particularly nice in the little red cap her grandmother made for her. She is so young and *naive* she trusts the wolf.

1. A *hood* is _____ (n).
      a) a head covering   b) a jacket   c) boots
    (*Note:* Think about the hood of your car, the hood over your stove, the hood of a cobra!)

2. *Naive* means _____(adj).
      a) smart   b) innocent   c) brave

Clue 2

Her mother tells her to take a *basket* of wine and cake, go straight to her grandmother, and not to *loiter*.

3. A *basket* is _____(n).
      a) a bag   b) a backpack   c) a container

4. *Loiter* means _____ (v).
      a) to stand around   b) to throw garbage   c) to move quickly

Clue 3

The wolf was so very hungry that he *leaped* and *sprang* on the bed to reach the grandmother and *gobbled* her up in no time.

5. *Leap* means _____(v).
      a) to jump high   b) to fall   c) to eat

6. *Sprang* (past tense of *spring*) means _____(v).
      a) opposite of autumn   b) to jump quickly   c) a metal spiral

7. *Gobble* means _____(v).
      a) to drink   b) to chew   c) to eat quickly

Clue 4

The wolf tells Little Red Riding Hood to look happy and not so *solemn*. Then she gathers a big *bunch* of flowers.

8. *Solemn* means _____(adj).
      a) serious   b) happy   c) silly

9. A *bunch* is _____(n).
    a) a little   b) a group   c) a plant

Clue 5

When the wolf knocks on the door, he *imitates* the voice of Little Red Riding Hood. The grandmother is in bed, so the wolf has to let himself in the locked door by lifting the *latch*.

10. *Imitate* means _____ (v).
    a) to begin   b) to laugh at   c) to copy

11. A *latch* is _____ (n).
    a) a lock   b) a straw roof   c) a key

Questions for Discussion

First, reread the story carefully looking for the deeper meanings and reviewing the vocabulary. Then in groups of four discuss the following questions with your classmates. Be sure to tell what your native culture is.
1. What was your favorite sentence in this story and why?
2. Which ending do you prefer and why?
3. Which ending teaches the better lesson and why?
4. Do you think that Little Red Riding Hood deserved to die as she did in the original version?

Putting All the Pieces Together

Look at the puzzles on page 18 and page 23. Find the pieces that fit this story and discuss what cultural values this folktale teaches American children.

Double-checking the Vocabulary

Fill in the crossword with the following vocabulary words: hood, loiter, naive, basket, solemn, bunch, imitate, leap, gobble, latch, spring.

Across

1. a simple fastening for a lock, usually dropping a bar into a U-shaped space
2. to eat fast
3. to jump quickly
4. innocent
5. to stand around doing nothing
6. a container, usually made of straw

Down

7. serious
8. a top or cover
9. a number of things held together
10. to jump high
11. to copy

Writing

Think, *in English*, about the most similar story in your culture. Then, using the vocabulary words, write it, *in English*, in correct American form and as briefly as possible.

Speaking

Now, tell your story.

Beauty and the Beast

Reading Readiness

A. With a partner look at this advertisement. Describe what you see. Try to guess the names of the characters in the story and what the story will be about.
B. Look at these questions and share your ideas with the class.
   1. Do you believe that beauty is only skin deep?
   2. Could you fall in love with a very ugly person?

Has Acid Indigestion Turned Your Stomach into a Beast?

Try

Guaranteed to Turn Your Stomach from a Hideous Monster into a Beauty

(Available without a Prescription)

Background Notes

This story has an ancient theme found in stories throughout the world in which a young, beautiful girl is forced to marry a monster. This particular story was written in French by Madame LePrince de Beaumont in 1756, and it was translated into English in 1761. It was made into an animated musical by Walt Disney in 1993. You might want to watch the video after you read the story.

Reading Selection

Now read this story once, as quickly as possible, for the general idea. Try to guess the meanings of the words you don't understand by the context. You can underline the words you don't know, but don't stop reading.

There was once a very rich merchant who had six children, three sons and three daughters. He gave his daughters everything they wanted, and they were very conceited and spoiled, except for the youngest, whom they called Beauty. She was as beautiful as she was sweet, and her two sisters were very jealous of her.

One terrible day the merchant learned that he had lost all of his money, and the family was forced to move from their rich mansion in town to a small house in the country. The sons immediately helped their father with the outside chores. Poor Beauty, she had never lived without servants. Now she had to get up before sunrise to light the fire and make the food and clean the house. But she soon got used to it and said, "Crying won't make it better. I must try to make myself happy." Her sisters stayed in bed till noon and were angry that Beauty was not as miserable as they.

A year later, the father received a letter that one of his lost ships had been found and had arrived filled with merchandise for him. Everyone was delighted, for they would once again be rich. As the merchant left, the two older daughters begged their father to bring them home all sorts of jewels and gowns. "And what does my Beauty want?" the father asked. "Oh, I need nothing, but if you could bring me a rose, that would be so nice," she said. Now, Beauty did not need the rose, but she thought she had better ask for something so as not to criticize her sisters' greed.

The merchant reached the harbor, but alas, the vessel had sunk and he was still as poor as before. On the way home he got lost in a forest, and it began to snow. "I shall die of the cold or be eaten by wolves and never see my dear children again," he thought. Suddenly, he saw a large house with all the lights on. He knocked at the door, but no one answered. He entered to find a large fire burning in the fireplace and a table set with delicious food. He waited a long time for the owner to appear, but no one came. He was starving, and he finally ate a bit of the food. He then found a bedroom and fell fast asleep. The next morning he was astonished to find a new suit of clothes set out for him and a fresh breakfast awaiting him. "This must be the castle of some fairies," he thought, and so he said a loud "thank you" and left. He was surprised to see that the snow had disappeared and that there was a lovely garden filled with rosebushes. "I shall take just one rose for my Beauty," he said, but as he cut the rose he heard a loud and terrible voice. He saw a most hideous monster who said, "Ungrateful man! I have saved your life and in return you steal my roses. You must die!" But the merchant beseeched him for the sake of his children. The Beast seemed interested when he learned of Beauty and her request for the rose. "Then you must ask her to come in place of you. You will have three months. Return home, and if she will not come then you must return. But you will not depart empty-handed. Return to your room and you will find a chest of gold," the Beast said. "Well, if I must die, at least I shall not leave my children destitute," thought the father, and he took the chest of gold and returned home.

"Here, Beauty," he said, "take this rose. Little do you know how that rose will cost your unhappy father his life." And he related his adventure with the monster.

Beauty immediately insisted on returning to the home of the Beast to save her father's life and would hear no arguments. On the day of her departure her sisters rubbed their eyes with onions, pretending to be sad that she was leaving and would probably die.

When the merchant and Beauty arrived at the palace, it was lit exactly as before. The fire was roaring and the table set splendidly. "Oh, the Beast intends to fatten me before he kills me," thought Beauty, but she acted cheerful and brave for her father. Suddenly they heard a horrible noise, and the monster appeared. "Have you come here willingly?" the monster asked. "Yes," trembled Beauty. "Good, then say farewell to your father." And the grief-stricken merchant had to leave his daughter and return home.

Beauty was sure that the Beast would eat her that night. She was surprised to find "Beauty's Apartment" engraved on a gold plate over the door of her bedroom. The room was full of magnificent furniture and the books that she loved. There was a piano for her to play. Inside one of the books was written,

Welcome Beauty, banish fear,
You are queen and mistress here.
Speak your wishes, speak your will,
Swift obedience meets them still.

"With all this magnificence, I don't suppose the Beast will eat me soon," she said, and felt less afraid.

The next night the Beast came to the dinner table and said, "Beauty, will you let me watch you eat? You are the mistress here. If my presence bothers you I will leave. Tell me, do you think I am very ugly?" And Beauty said, "Yes," because she could not lie, but she added, "but I think you are very good-natured." They talked, and Beauty started to feel very calm until the monster said, "Beauty will you be my wife?" She did not want to make the monster angry, but she said, "No." The monster began to howl and sadly said, "Then, farewell, Beauty," and left the room.

For three months the same thing happened each night at dinner. Beauty began to look forward to these visits and lost her fear of the monster's deformity, but every night, before he left, he asked the same question: "Beauty, will you be my wife?"

"Oh, Beast, I wish I could consent to marry you. I shall always consider you a great friend, but I do not love you."

"But will you promise to never leave me?" the Beast asked.

"Oh, Beast, I am so worried about my dear father, and I miss him so."

"Ah, then you will leave, and the Beast will die of grief."

"Oh, no," said Beauty. "If you let me visit my father, I promise I will return and live with you forever."

"You shall be there tomorrow," said the Beast. "But remember, when you wish to return to me, you must lay your ring on the table before you go to bed."

The next morning, when Beauty awoke, she found herself in her father's home, and her room was filled with chests of gold and gowns from the Beast. Everyone was overjoyed to see her except her sisters. They were consumed with jealousy, but they pretended to be happy and begged her to stay as long as she could. On the tenth night Beauty had a dream in which she saw the Beast lying in his garden, dying. She awoke in tears. "Oh, how ungrateful I am. Is it his fault that he is so very ugly? He has been so kind and generous to me. Why did I not consent to marry him?" Then she got out of bed, put her ring on the table, and went back to sleep. The next morning she awoke in the Beast's castle. She put on her most beautiful gown and waited for him to come. After dinner, when he still hadn't appeared, she remembered the dream and ran to the garden, where she found him lying on the ground, almost dead. She bent over him, crying and hugging him. "Oh, Beast, please do not die! Live and be my husband." At those words she saw bright flashes of light and heard music, and, instead of the hideous beast, she saw one of the loveliest princes that eyes ever saw. He thanked her for putting an end to the horrible spell that had been cast over him by a wicked witch. Then a fairy appeared waving a wand, and Beauty's entire family appeared. The fairy smiled and said, "Beauty, you have made a wise choice, for you have chosen virtue over beauty. You and the prince shall live a very happy life." Then the fairy turned to Beauty's two sisters and said, "You who are so consumed by envy and jealousy, you will become two statues but still retain your reason. You will stand at the door of Beauty's castle, and it will be your punishment to observe her daily happiness until the day you die."

Checking Your Comprehension

Answer these questions in class.
1. Why does the Beast threaten to kill the merchant?
2. Why does the Beast not kill the merchant?
3. Why does Beauty decide to marry the Beast?
4. Why does the fairy turn the sisters into statues?

Be a Vocabulary Detective

Working in pairs, look for hints and guess the vocabulary from the context clues. Then fill in the blanks with the correct answers.

Clue 1

The merchant has given his *spoiled* daughters everything they want, and yet they are *ungrateful*. When they become poor, the two older sisters will not help Beauty with her household *chores*.

1. *Spoiled* means_____ (adj).
   a) sweet   b) self-centered   c) dirty

2. *Ungrateful* is _____ (adj).
   a) unappreciative   b) content   c) rich

3. A *chore* is _____ (n).
   a) a cookie   b) a small job   c) the sand near the sea

Clue 2

The merchant goes to the *harbor* to unload his merchandise from the ship only to find that the boat and all his money have been lost and he is *destitute*.

4. A *harbor* is _____(n).
   a) a store   b) a famous college   c) a safe place in the water

5. To be *destitute* means _____ (adj).
   a) to be rich   b) to be very poor c) to be middle class

Clue 3

When the merchant meets the Beast, he is so afraid that he *trembles* because the Beast is so *hideous*. The Beast is extremely ugly and misshapen. The merchant is afraid of the Beast's *deformity*.

6. *Tremble* means_____(v).
   a) to shake   b) to cry   c) to run

7. *Hideous* means _____ (adj).
   a) beautiful   b) hidden   c) extremely ugly

8. A *deformity* is _____(n).
   a) a piece of furniture b) an abnormality c) a surprise

Clue 4

The Beast *beseeches* Beauty to marry him, and when she says, "No," he *howls* with unhappiness.

9. *Beseech* means_____(v).
   a) to beg   b) to look for c) to argue with

10. *Howl* means _____(v).
    a) to question   b) to make a loud, sad noise c) to sob

Clue 5

"Beauty's Apartment" is *engraved* on a gold plate over her door. She reads a poem that tells her to relax and *banish* fear.

11. *Engrave* means _____(v).
    a) to put in the earth b) to write on metal c) to be very serious

12. *Banish* means _____(v).
    a) to get rid of b) to end   c) to shine

Clue 6

The fairy is pleased with Beauty's *virtue* because she made a good choice when she decided to marry the ugly Beast because of his kindness.

13. *Virtue* is _____ (n).
    a) vice   b) weakness   c) goodness

Questions for Discussion

First, reread the story carefully looking for the deeper meanings and reviewing the vocabulary. Then in groups of four discuss the following questions with your classmates. Be sure to tell what your native culture is.

1. What was your favorite sentence in this story and why?
2. Would you have made the two sacrifices that Beauty made?
3. Did the sisters deserve their punishment?

Putting All the Pieces Together

Look at the puzzles on page 18 and page 23. Find the pieces that fit this story and discuss what cultural values this folktale teaches American children.

Double-checking the Vocabulary

Match the definitions with the words.

a.	completely without money	1. spoil
b.	to shake uncontrollably	2. chores
c.	to stop thinking about; to remove	3. harbor
d.	to make a child selfish from having too much attention	4. hideous
e.	a long, loud cry of pain or anger	5. ungrateful
f.	household jobs	6. beseech
g.	goodness; the opposite of vice	7. destitute
h.	to beg	8. tremble
i.	a severe imperfection of the body	9. engrave
j.	not showing thanks or appreciation	10. banish
k.	to cut words or pictures on wood, stone, or metal	11. howl
l.	shocking to the eyes	12. deformity
m.	a sheltered area of water where ships are safe	13. virtue

Writing

Think, *in English*, about the most similar story in your culture. Then, using the vocabulary words, write it, *in English*, in correct American form and as briefly as possible.

Speaking

Now, tell your story.

Rip Van Winkle

Reading Readiness

A. With a partner look at this advertisement. Describe what you see. Try to guess the names of the characters in the story and what the story will be about.

Having Trouble Falling Asleep?

Try **Rip Van Winkle Sleep Tabs**

Guaranteed Safe and Fast Acting. No Side Effects: Wake up Refreshed and Alert, Yet as Rested as If You Had Slept for 20 Years. Non-addictive; All Natural Ingredients. Available at All Fine Pharmacies

B. Look at these questions and share your ideas with the class.
1. Have you ever awakened in the morning and felt that everything seemed strange and changed?
2. If there were a "time machine" but it only had *one way* tickets, would you buy one and leave the present so that you could travel to the future?

Background Notes

This story about a man named Rip (who doesn't do a lot of work around the house), his angry wife, some strange men who give Rip something special to drink, and what happens when Rip wakes up was based on an old traditional German tale. It was written by the *first* professional author of the new American Republic, Washington Irving. This story was first published in 1819.

Reading Selection

Now read this story once, as quickly as possible, for the general idea. Try to guess the meanings of the words you don't understand by the context. You can under-line the words you don't know, but don't stop reading.

Many years ago, when America was still a colony of England, in the Catskill Mountains of the Hudson River there was a little village of great antiquity that had been built by Dutch colonists in 1626. In that village there lived a simple, good-natured fellow named Rip Van Winkle. He was a kind neighbor and an obedient, henpecked husband. Everyone in the village loved Rip Van Winkle. The good wives took his part in his family squabbles and would put all the blame on Mrs. Van Winkle. The children of the village, too, would shout with joy whenever Rip approached. He would help them with their sports, teach them to fly kites, and tell them long stories of ghosts and witches. Not even a dog would bark as Rip walked past.

The great problem in Rip's character was an inability to support his family. It wasn't that he was lazy, for he could sit on a wet rock and fish all day without even catching a fish. He could hunt all day, walking through the wet forest, even if he did not bring home any food. He never refused to help a neighbor in even the most difficult work, and he was the hardest worker at building stone fences, running errands for the women, etc. In a word, Rip was ready to do anybody's business but his own, and he found keeping his own farm in order to be impossible. The fences were always falling down, the cows would get lost, nothing would grow on the land. His children, too, were as ragged and wild as the farm.

Rip Van Winkle, however, was one of those happy mortals who take the world easy. He would have been perfectly content, but his wife continually nagged him. Morning, noon, and night her tongue was incessantly going, and everything he said or did would cause her to complain. Rip always replied in the same way. He shrugged his shoulders, shook his head, rolled up his eyes, and said nothing. This would produce more complaints from his wife, and so he was forced to take to the outside—the only side that belongs to a henpecked husband.

Times grew worse and worse with Rip Van Winkle as the years of marriage rolled on. A hot temper never cools with age, and a sharp tongue is the only knife that grows sharper with constant use.

Poor Rip was at last reduced almost to despair, and his only alternative was to take his gun and stroll away into the woods with his only friend, his dog, Wolf, who was as henpecked as his master. "Poor Wolf," Rip would say, "Mrs. Van Winkle gives you a dog's life of it. But never mind, while I live you shall never need a friend to stand by you." Wolf would wag his tail, and, if dogs can feel pity, I believe he did.

One fine autumn day, Rip had climbed to the highest parts of the Catskill Mountains. Looking down he could see the majestic Hudson River and the sleeping valleys below. It would soon be dark, so he began to climb down. Then he suddenly heard a voice calling, "Rip Van Winkle! Rip Van Winkle!" At the same time Wolf gave a low growl and looked fearfully around. Rip also felt afraid. He saw a strange figure walking toward him. Surprised to see anyone in this lonely and unfrequented place, Rip was even more surprised at the stranger's appearance. The stranger was a short man with a thick bushy beard, wearing a style of clothing of the Dutch fashion of a hundred years ago. On his back he had a heavy keg that seemed full of liquor. He made signs for Rip to come with him. Although afraid, Rip followed. He could hear the rumbling of distant thunder, and at length they came to a flat area where Rip saw nine strange-looking men, bowling. They all wore antique Dutch clothing and seemed very silent and sad. The only sound was that of the bowling ball knocking down the pins.

The strange men immediately stopped playing when they saw Rip and made signs to him to join them in drinking. Rip, who was a naturally thirsty soul, eagerly tasted the beverage, which had the flavor of Holland gin. One taste led to another, and at last his senses were overpowered, his eyes swam in his head, his head gradually lowered, and he fell into a deep sleep.

On waking he rubbed his eyes—it was a bright sunny morning. "Surely," thought Rip, "I have not slept all night! Oh, what excuse will I make to my wife?" He looked for his gun but could only find an old rusted gun with the wooden handle eaten by worms. Wolf, too, had disappeared. Rip whistled and shouted, but no dog was to be seen. Everything looked so different. There was a mountain stream he had never seen before. He whistled again for Wolf. What was to be done? He missed his dog and couldn't find his gun. He dreaded to meet his wife, but he was famished. He didn't want to starve among the mountains, so he shook his head and, with a heart full of trouble, turned his steps homeward.

As he approached his village, he met a number of people he had never seen before, and to his surprise, they were wearing a different style of clothing. They stared at his face and touched their chins. This made Rip do the same, and he was astonished to find that his beard had grown a foot long! As he entered the village all was changed. It was larger, and there were more people. Strange names were over the doors and strange faces in the windows. "That liquor last night has really confused my poor head," thought Rip.

He was able to find his way to his house and saw that it was empty and abandoned. The roof had fallen in, the windows were all shattered, and the doors were all open. A dog that looked like Wolf growled and showed his teeth. "My very dog has forgotten me!" sighed Rip. He then went to the town tavern and was shocked to see on the sign, not the red face of King George III, but a portrait of a stranger with the words "General Washington." Inside the people were talking about Congress, liberty, the heroes of '76, and the election. As Rip entered the tavern all conversation stopped. "Who are you voting for? Are you a Federal or a Democrat?" they asked. "I am a poor quiet man, a native of this place, and a loyal subject of King George, God bless him!" Rip said. "A spy, a spy!" they all screamed. "Take him away." Rip insisted that he was an honest man and had come only to find his friends. When he mentioned their names, his heart sank, for he was told that they had died or had gone off to Congress. "Does nobody here know Rip Van Winkle?" "Oh, Rip Van Winkle. Yes, he's over there leaning against that tree." Rip looked and saw himself as if looking in a mirror. Then a young woman with a crying child came to look at the strange old man. "Hush, Rip," she said to the child. "The old man won't hurt you." "What is your name, my good woman?" asked Rip. "Judith Gardenier." "And your father's name?" "Ah, poor man, Rip Van Winkle was his name, but it's twenty years since he went away from home with only his gun and has never been heard of since. His dog came home without him, and whether he shot himself or was carried off nobody can tell. I was then but a little girl. That's my brother leaning against the tree." "Where's your mother?" "Oh, she died a short time after. She broke a blood vessel in an argument with a store clerk."

There was a drop of comfort, at least, in this news. Rip could contain himself no longer. He caught his daughter and grandchild in his arms and said, "I am your father!" An old woman seeing his face said, "Sure enough, it is Rip Van Winkle—it is himself. Where have you been these twenty years?" After Rip told his story, the oldest man in the village was called, and he said that the Catskill Mountains had been haunted by strange beings, the ghosts of the great Dutch explorer Hendrick Hudson and his crew of the ship the *Half-Moon*, who always kept an eye on the river and land they had discovered.

To make a long story short, Rip's daughter took him home with her, and Rip and his tale became famous throughout the village.

Even to this day, when the people of that village hear thunder, they say that it is Hendrick Hudson and his crew bowling in the Catskills. And many a henpecked husband wishes he could have a taste of that Holland gin.

Checking Your Comprehension

Answer these questions in class.
1. Why is Mrs. Van Winkle always angry at her husband?
2. Why does Rip climb up to the top of the Catskill Mountains?
3. Why does no one recognize Rip when he comes home?

Be a Vocabulary Detective

Working in pairs, look for hints and guess the vocabulary from the context clues. Then fill in the blanks with the correct answers.

Clue 1

Poor Rip is a *henpecked* husband. Mrs. Van Winkle is always angry with him. She criticizes him constantly, she talks *incessantly*, she is always *nagging* him and won't stop telling him what to do. But the other wives of the village agree with Rip in those *squabbles*.

1. *Henpecked* means _____ (adj).
   a) told what to do   b) adored   c) eating eggs

2. *Incessantly* means _____ (adv).
   a) never   b) sometimes   c) all the time

3. *Nag* means _____ (v).
   a) to eat   b) to criticize   c) an old horse

4. A *squabble* is _____ (n).
   a) a cooked chicken   b) an argument   c) a party

Clue 2

When Mrs. Van Winkle talks, Rip just *shrugs* his shoulders and pretends that he doesn't understand. He leaves the house and *strolls* in the woods with his only friend, his dog, Wolf. Wolf loves his master and always *wags* his tail. He would never *growl* at Rip; he only growls at enemies. After the liquor, when Rip wakes up, his dog is gone and Rip *dreads* going home.

5. *Shrug* means _____(v).
   a) to shake   b) to move the shoulders   c) to laugh

6. *Stroll* means _____ (v).
   a) to take a slow walk   b) to push a baby   c) to run

7. *Wag* means_____ (v).
   a) to sit   b) to move back and forth   c) to criticize

8. *Growl* means_____ (v).
   a) to giggle   b) to cry   c) to make a low, angry sound

9. *Dread* means _____ (v).
   a) to fear   b) to look forward to   c) to die

Clue 3

When Rip meets the strange men in the mountain, he thinks he hears thunder, but it is just the men *bowling* with a ball and pins. After he drinks their liquor he falls asleep and wakes to find his gun all *rusted* and useless.

10. *Bowling* is _____ (n).
    a) a round plate   b) a sport   c) an argument

11. *Rusted* is _____ (adj).
    a) cooked in an oven b) full of red dust from age   c) broken

Clue 4

Rip's village is of great *antiquity,* and the costumes of the strange men are also very old.

12. *Antiquity* means _____ (n).
    a) oldness   b) expense   c) newness

Questions for Discussion

First, reread the story carefully looking for the deeper meanings and reviewing the vocabulary. Then in groups of four discuss the following questions with your classmates. Be sure to tell what your native culture is.
1. What was your favorite sentence in this story and why?
2. Do you think that Mrs. Van Winkle had a right to complain about Rip?
3. Why did the ghosts of Hendrick Hudson call out Rip's name and invite him to drink with them?

Putting All the Pieces Together

Look at the puzzles on page 18 and page 23. Find the pieces that fit this story and discuss what cultural values this folktale teaches American children.

Double-checking the Vocabulary

Fill in the crossword puzzle with the following vocabulary words: antiquity, henpecked, squabbles, nag, incessantly, shrug, stroll, wag, growl, bowling, rust, dread. You will also need the word *us*.

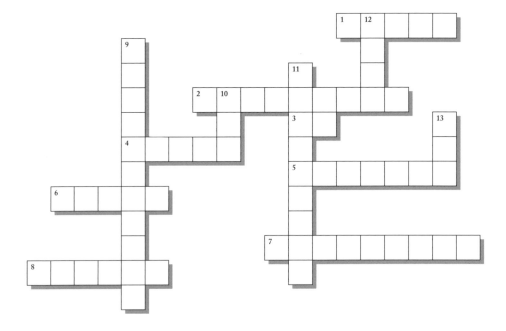

Across

1. a deep rough sound, often from an animal
2. the quality of being exceedingly old, from the past
3. a synonym for "we"
4. to raise one's shoulders, often in a question
5. a game played with a large, round, heavy ball that attempts to knock down bottle-shaped wooden objects
6. to fear greatly
7. scolded by one's wife and obedient to her
8. a long, easy walk

Down

9. constantly, without stopping
10. to complain continuously
11. arguments over something unimportant
12. the reddish brown surface that forms on iron when it is exposed to water and air
13. shake a part of the body quickly from side to side

Writing

Think, *in English*, about the most similar story in your culture. Then, using the vocabulary words, write it, *in English*, in correct American form and as briefly as possible.

Speaking

Now, tell your story.

Chapter  6

Love Conquers All

Love conquers all things, let us surrender to love.
—Virgil, 70-19 B.C.

It's love, it's love, that makes the world go round.
—Old French Song

The magic of first love is our ignorance that it can ever end.
—Benjamin Disraeli 1804-81

Snow White

Reading Readiness

A. With a partner look at this advertisement. Describe what you see. Try to guess the names of the characters in the story and what the story will be about.

B. Look at these questions and share your ideas with the class.
   1. Can you imagine being so jealous of someone you wished that person were dead? How would it feel? What would you do?
   2. Do you believe in love at first sight?

Mirror Mirror on the Wall

No More Ugly Distortions When You Look at Yourself in a Snow White Mirror

Guaranteed to Reflect Yourself Accurately. You Will Be Assured of Being the Fairest in the Land. What You See Will Be the Truth!

Call Snow White Mirrors 1-800-MIRRORS

Background Notes

This folk story, collected by the Brothers Grimm, about a little princess who is so beautiful that her stepmother is jealous of her beauty and tries to kill her has been found in different versions throughout Europe, and also in Asia and parts of North Africa. The tale was made extremely popular in the United States after Walt Disney made it into one of his first animated films in 1938. In that film, he gave names to the Seven Dwarfs. You might want to see the video after you read this story.

Reading Selection

Now read this story once, as quickly as possible, for the general idea. Try to guess the meanings of the words you don't understand by the context. You can underline the words you don't know, but don't stop reading.

Once, in the middle of winter, a beautiful young queen sat sewing at the window. The ebony frame of the window was open, and she was looking at the snowflakes falling like feathers. Suddenly, she pricked her finger, and three drops of blood fell out onto the snow. "Oh, if only I had a little child as white as snow, as red as blood, and as black as that ebony window." Soon after, a beautiful little daughter was born to the queen. The child's skin was as white as the snow. Her lips were as red as blood and her hair as black as ebony. They called her Snow White. But the good queen died soon after the birth of the child. The king married another wife, who was very beautiful but very vain about her beauty. She could not tolerate anyone being more beautiful than she. She had a magical mirror into which she would gaze and say,

> Mirror, Mirror, on the wall,
> Who's the fairest of them all?

And the magic mirror would always say,

> Thou, my queen, are fairest in the land.

And she would be happy because the mirror never lied.
When Snow White was seven, her beauty became famous throughout the kingdom. Then one day the queen went to ask the mirror,

> Mirror, Mirror, on the wall,
> Who's the fairest of them all?

This time the magic mirror said,

> Thou, my queen, have beauty quite rare,
> But Snow White is a thousand times more fair.

The queen became enraged and turned green with envy. She called for her huntsman and said, "Take the child far into the forest and kill her. And bring me back her heart as proof." The huntsman took Snow White into the forest and pulled a large knife out of its case, but the child began to weep. The huntsman took pity and let her run away. He killed a deer and brought back its heart, which the queen cooked and ate.

Meanwhile, the frightened child wandered all alone in the dark forest. She ran and ran and suddenly came upon a clearing with a little house. She knocked, but no one was home, and, finding the door unlocked, she went in. Everything inside was extremely clean and tidy, and everything was very tiny. There was a table with a sparkling white tablecloth and seven little plates. Each plate had a little spoon and knife and fork and a little tiny cup. Against the wall were seven little beds. Snow White was very hungry, but she didn't want to take what was not hers, so she took a tiny crumb from the bread on each plate and a little drop of wine from each cup. Then she tried out the beds to see which one was best. Finally she chose the seventh bed and fell fast asleep.

At dusk, the owners of the cottage came home. They were seven little dwarfs who worked in the mountains mining for gold and jewels. They immediately noticed that something was wrong. "Someone's been sitting in my chair," said the first dwarf. "Someone's been eating my bread," said the second dwarf. "Someone's been touching my knife," said the third dwarf. "Someone's been touching my fork," said the fourth dwarf. "Someone's been touching my spoon," said the fifth dwarf. "Someone's been drinking my wine," said the sixth dwarf. "Someone's moved my plate," said the seventh dwarf. Then they noticed that someone had been lying in their beds, and the seventh dwarf saw Snow White asleep in his.

She was such a beautiful child that they didn't want to wake her so the seventh dwarf shared the beds of the others throughout that night.

In the morning the little girl awoke and was very frightened when she saw the seven little men. But they seemed so kind that she told them her story. "If you'll keep house for us and clean and sweep and cook and make everything neat, you may stay here with us," they said. "But you must beware of your wicked stepmother because she may try to kill you again." And so Snow White and the seven dwarfs lived happily together.

The queen was quite convinced she was the most beautiful in the land, but a few years later she went again to the mirror to check.

Mirror, Mirror, on the wall,
Who's the fairest of them all?

And the mirror answered,

Thou, my queen, have beauty quite rare,
But with the seven dwarfs quite far away
Lives Snow White, and I must say
She is still a thousand times more fair.

The queen became horrified because she knew the mirror never lied. She disguised herself as an old peddler, put ribbons and laces in a basket, and went into the forest and across the mountains to the little house of the seven dwarfs. She knocked on the door. "Pretty things for sale, pretty things for sale." Snow White felt that this must be an honest old woman and let her in. "Oh, my dear, you need new laces for your dress!" (In those days women wore tight laces on their dresses to make their waists look smaller.) And the wicked queen laced Snow White so tightly that she lost her breath and fell down as if dead. Not long after, the dwarfs came home to find their beloved Snow White lying on the floor. They immediately saw the problem, cut the laces, and she began to breathe again. "That old peddler was the wicked queen. You must promise not to let anyone in the house," they warned her.

When the evil queen went home she immediately went to the mirror and said,

Mirror, Mirror, on the wall,
Who's the fairest of them all?

And the mirror answered,

Thou, my queen, have beauty quite rare,
But with the seven dwarfs quite far away
Lives Snow White still, and I must say
She is a thousand times more fair.

The queen's heart began to pound with anger, and she could not eat or sleep until she could think of a way to kill Snow White. This time she disguised herself as an old woman and put a poison comb in a basket. Then she went into the forest and across the mountains to the little house of the seven dwarfs. She knocked on the door. "Pretty things for sale, pretty things for sale." Snow White looked out the window and said, "Go away. I'm not allowed to let anyone in." "But of course you can look," said the queen, lifting the beautiful comb up to the window. The comb was so beautiful that Snow White put it in her hair. Immediately she fell down as if dead. Not long after, the dwarfs came home to find their beloved Snow White lying on the floor. They immediately saw the problem, removed the comb, and she opened her eyes. "That old woman was the wicked queen. You must promise to be more careful."

When the evil queen went home she rushed to the mirror and said,

Mirror, Mirror on the wall,
Who's the fairest of them all?

And the mirror answered,

Thou, my queen, have beauty quite rare,
But with the seven dwarfs quite far away
Lives Snow White still, and I must say
She is a thousand times more fair.

The queen trembled with rage. "Snow White must die!" She went to a secret place in the castle and mixed up a strong poison. Then she dipped an apple into it, put on the disguise of an old beggar woman, put the apple in the basket, and went into the forest and across the mountains to the cottage of the seven dwarfs. She knocked on the door. "Apples for sale, apples for sale." Snow White looked out the window and said, "Go away! I'm not allowed to let anyone in." "But let me give you a gift of an apple. They are so very delicious," said the queen, lifting up the beautiful apple to the window. "No, I can't," said Snow White. "Are you afraid it is poison?" asked the queen and she took a bite of the apple, for it was very special and had the poison only on one side. She gave the other side to Snow White, who couldn't resist and took a bite. Immediately she fell down dead.

The queen rushed home to the mirror and asked,

Mirror, Mirror on the wall,
Who's the fairest of them all?

And this time the magic mirror said,

> Thou, my queen, are now the fairest in the land.

And she was very happy.

When the dwarfs came home they found their beloved Snow White lying on the floor dead. Try as they would, they could not revive her. They sat beside her for three days weeping and lamenting. When it was time to bury her, her lips were still as red as blood, and they couldn't think of putting her into the cold ground. They built a coffin of glass and gently laid her in it. They carried the coffin to the top of the mountain and placed a sign on it, "Here lies Snow White, a king's daughter." The dwarfs took turns guarding it at all times.

Many years later a prince was traveling through the forest and spent the night at the little house of the seven dwarfs. The next morning they took him to see the coffin of Snow White, and he immediately fell in love with her. "Let me have the coffin. I will pay you whatever you ask," he begged. But the dwarfs said they wouldn't sell it for all the gold in the world. "Then give it to me as a gift. I won't be able to go on living without her." The dwarfs agreed. As the prince's servants were moving the coffin onto a horse, the coffin slipped, and that forced the piece of poisoned apple out of Snow White's throat. She opened her eyes and saw the handsome prince. "Where am I? What happened?" she asked. The prince immediately asked her to marry him and she said yes.

Now it happened that Snow White's stepmother was invited to the wedding of the prince and his mysterious princess, and as she was dressing she went to her mirror and asked,

> Mirror, Mirror, on the wall,
> Who's the fairest of them all?

And the magic mirror said,

> Thou, my queen, have beauty quite rare,
> But the bride, Snow White, is a thousand times more fair.

The evil queen didn't know what to do. She went to the wedding, and yes, indeed, Snow White was the bride. But they had prepared for the wicked stepmother. They caused iron shoes to be heated and put on her feet, and she had to dance in them until she fell down dead.

As for Snow White and the prince, well, they lived happily ever after.

Checking Your Comprehension

Answer these questions in class.
1. Why does the stepmother hate Snow White?
2. Why don't the dwarfs bury Snow White in the ground?
3. How does Snow White come back to life?

Be a Vocabulary Detective

Working in pairs, look for hints and guess the vocabulary from the context clues. Then fill in the blanks with the correct answers.

Clue 1

The young queen is sewing in front of a window frame made of *ebony*. As she sews, the needle *pricks* her finger, and blood comes out.

1. *Ebony* is _____ (n).
   a) glass   b) plastic   c) a black wood

2. *Prick* means _____ (v).
   a) to stick   b) to kiss   c) to sew

Clue 2

The stepmother is a very jealous woman. She is so *vain* that she feels she is the most beautiful woman in the kingdom, and she cannot *tolerate* the fact that anyone could be better than she. She feels deep *envy* when she finds that Snow White is more beautiful. She becomes so *enraged* that she *trembles*.

3. *Vain* means _____ (adj).
   a) humble   b) sweet   c) conceited

4. *Tolerate* is _____ (v).
   a) to hate   b) to sing   c) to allow

5. *Envy* means_____ (n).
   a) jealousy   b) love   c) hunger

6. To be *enraged* means _____ (adj).
   a) to be angry   b) to be happy   c) to be sad

7. *Tremble* is _____ (v).
   a) to dance   b) to laugh   c) to shake

Clue 3

The seven *dwarfs* live in a cottage that is very clean and *tidy*. They take *pity* on the little girl and offer to take care of her.

8. A *dwarf* is _____ (n).
   a) an animal   b) a child   c) a small person

9. *Tidy* is _____ (adj).
   a) messy   b) organized   c) dirty

10. *Take pity* is _____ (v).
    a) to feel anger   b) to feel sorry for   c) to feel jealous

Clue 4

The wicked queen plans to kill Snow White. She puts on a *disguise* and pretends to be a *peddler*.

11. A *disguise* is_____(n).
    a) a costume   b) a pretty dress   c) boots

12. A *peddler* is _____(n).
    a) a salesperson   b) a bicyclist   c) a waiter

Clue 5

The magic mirror is very old and speaks a very old English. It says "*Thou*, my queen, are fairest in the land."

13. *Thou* means_____ (pron).
    a) we   b) she   c) you (singular)

Questions for Discussion

First, reread the story carefully looking for the deeper meanings and reviewing the vocabulary. Then in groups of four discuss the following questions with your classmates. Be sure to tell what your native culture is.

1. What was your favorite sentence in this story and why?
2. Is Snow White responsible for the bad things that happened to her?
3. Do you think that the stepmother deserved her end?

Putting All the Pieces Together

Look at the puzzles on page 18 and page 23. Find the pieces that fit this story and discuss what cultural values this folktale teaches American children.

Double-checking the Vocabulary

Fill in the crossword with the following vocabulary words: prick, ebony, vain, tolerate, thou, enraged, envy, to take pity, tidy, dwarf, peddler, disguise, tremble.

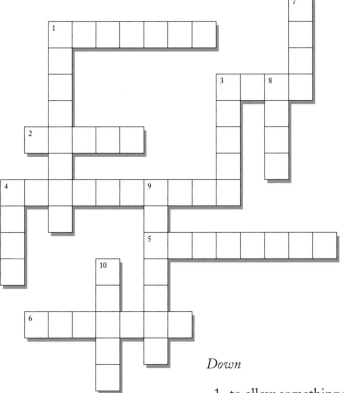

Down

1. to allow something you don't agree with to occur
3. a black wood
4. an old-fashioned way of saying "you"
7. very neat and organized
8. thinking too highly of yourself
9. someone who sells things door to door
10. a person of much less than the normal size

Across

1. to shake
2. to stick with a pin
3. jealousy
4. to feel sorry for someone (three words)
5. to change your appearance; to hide the way you look
6. to be filled with anger

Writing

Think, *in English*, about the most similar story in your culture. Then, using the vocabulary words, write it, *in English*, in correct American form and as briefly as possible.

Speaking

Now, tell your story to the class.

Rapunzel

Reading Readiness

A. With a partner look at this advertisement. Describe what you see. Try to guess the names of the characters in the story and what the story will be about.

Tired of Limp, Fragile Hair and Split Ends? Try Rapunzel Hair Care Shampoos and Protein Conditioners Guaranteed to Make Your Dull Hair So Strong and Glistening That Your Prince Will Be Ensnared.

Rapunzel Hair Care Products

B. Look at these questions and share your ideas with the class.
1. Should a good daughter leave the mother who has taken care of her and marry the man she loves (against the mother's wishes), or should she give up the man she loves?
2. When you make a deal with someone (promise that you will do something) is there ever a good reason to change your mind later and not keep your promise?

Background Notes

This is a very romantic folktale collected by the Brothers Grimm. It is about a young woman with extremely beautiful long, blond hair who is very lonely because her adopted mother forces her to live all by herself in a tower in a forest.

Reading Selection

Now read this story once, as quickly as possible, for the general idea. Try to guess the meanings of the words you don't understand by the context. You can underline the words you don't know, but don't stop reading.

Once there was a couple who had wanted to have a child for many, many years. Finally the wife became pregnant, and the man and woman were very happy. The wife would often look out the kitchen window into the garden next door. It was a splendid garden surrounded by a high wall, for their neighbor was a witch. As the wife looked into the garden she saw some delicious rapunzel lettuce growing. It made her mouth water, and she developed such a strong craving for that lettuce that she desired it more than anything else. She grew pale and unhappy. Her husband feared that she would die, and, because he loved her, when the sun set he climbed over the wall of the witch's garden, grabbed some rapunzel, and brought it to his wife. The rapunzel tasted so good that the wife craved it even more. So again the husband climbed the wall. But this time, just as he landed on the ground, he came face to face with the old witch. "How dare you come into my garden? Why do you steal my lettuce?" screamed the witch. "Oh, please, it is for my wife. She is with child and had such a craving for the rapunzel I feared she would die," said the good man. The witch softened. "All right. I shall let you have all the rapunzel she wants on one condition. When the child is born, you must give it to me. Have no fear. I will be a good mother." Because of his terror, the man agreed, and when a little daughter was born to them, the witch came to take the child away. They begged and cried and pleaded but to no avail.

The witch named the child Rapunzel, and she grew into the most beautiful child in the world. When she reached adolescence, the witch hid her in a tower that stood deep in the woods. It had neither staircase nor doors, only a little window high up in the wall.

When the witch wanted to enter the tower, she stood at the foot of it and cried, "Rapunzel, Rapunzel, let down your hair."

Rapunzel had splendid hair, twenty yards long, which was as fine as spun gold. When she heard the witch's voice, she would lower her braids out the window and the witch would climb up.

One day the king's son rode through that part of the forest and came close to the tower. He heard a song so lovely that he stopped to listen. It was Rapunzel singing. She was so lonely in the tower that she spent her days making up songs. The prince moved in closer and hid behind a tree. Soon he saw the witch come to the tower and call out, "Rapunzel, Rapunzel, let down your hair."

Rapunzel lowered her hair, and the witch climbed up.

The young prince waited until the witch left and then went to the bottom of the tower. "If that is the ladder, then I shall try my luck. Rapunzel, Rapunzel, let down your hair." The hair fell down at once, and he climbed up.

Rapunzel was quite frightened when the prince climbed through the window since she had never seen a man before. But he was so kind and spoke with such sincerity that she soon lost her fear. The prince talked with Rapunzel for many hours and told her of the world outside the tower. He told her of his love for her and asked for her hand.

She thought about it for a few moments and answered, "I am sure you will love me better than old Mother Witch. Yes, I will gladly go with you and be your wife, but I do not know how I am to get down from this tower."

Then Rapunzel had a wonderful idea. "When you come again, bring some silk. I will braid it into a ladder, and, when it is long enough, I will climb down and you can take me away on your horse." The prince said good-bye to Rapunzel and climbed down her hair. He planned to return at night for the witch only came in the day. But the next day Rapunzel said, "Oh Mother Witch, why does my scalp hurt so when you climb up, but the prince is so light, I don't feel any pull?" "Oh, so you have deceived me!" cried the witch. "You wicked child. I thought I had kept you from the world."

The old witch was so angry that she picked up a huge pair of scissors and cut Rapunzel's beautiful hair right off. She tied the hair to a hook, and they both climbed down. As soon as they were on the ground, the witch took Rapunzel away from the tower and forced her to live alone in a tiny cottage deep in the woods.

The witch hurried back to the tower and climbed up Rapunzel's hair and pulled it in after her. Then she waited silently for the prince to return. At dusk the prince rode up to the tower and called out, "Rapunzel, Rapunzel, let down your hair."

The witch threw the hair down and the prince climbed up. What he found was not his beloved Rapunzel but the ugly witch, who looked at him with angry and vicious eyes.

"So, you have come to fetch your love, but the pretty bird is no longer in her nest. She can sing no more. The cat has seized her, and it will scratch your eyes out too! Rapunzel is lost to you. You will never see her again."

The prince was so heartbroken that he leaped out of the tower window. He fell into a large bush covered with thorns. His eyes were scratched, and he was blinded. Sadly, he wandered about in the woods, unable to see, and wept for his lost love, Rapunzel.

He wandered for a whole year, eating only roots and berries, weeping for his lost wife. One day, he was very deep in the forest where Rapunzel was living with her twins, a boy and a girl. The prince heard a familiar voice singing. He went straight toward it, and Rapunzel recognized him immediately. She rushed to him and held him in her arms. "Oh, my beloved prince, I knew we would find each other at last." As she spoke, her tears fell into his eyes. Suddenly, the prince could see again as well as ever. Rapunzel's tears had restored his sight. Then the prince took Rapunzel and their children back to his kingdom, where they lived happily ever after.

Checking Your Comprehension

Answer these questions in class.
1. Why do the husband and wife give their child to the witch? Could they have done anything else?
2. Why and when does the witch lock Rapunzel in the tower?
3. What takes away the prince's blindness?

Be a Vocabulary Detective

Working in pairs, look for hints and guess the vocabulary from the context clues. Then fill in the blanks with the correct answers.

Clue 1

The wife is pregnant, and, like some women who are expecting babies, she has a *craving* for certain foods, particularly rapunzel lettuce, which *makes her mouth water*. When she can't have the rapunzel, she grows *pale* and ill.

1. *Crave* means _____ (v).
   a) to desire strongly   b) to dislike   c) to eat

2. To *make your mouth water* means _____ (idiom).
   a) to be bitter   b) to be temptingly delicious   c) to be thirsty

3. *Pale* means _____ (adj).
   a) cold   b) no color   c) weak

Clue 2

Rapunzel has *splendid* hair as *fine* as *spun gold* yet strong enough for someone to climb up. She wears it in long *braids* that the prince can climb like a ladder. But the witch is heavier and almost pulls Rapunzel's hair out of her *scalp*.

4. *Splendid* means _____ (adj).
   a) ugly   b) wonderful   c) expensive.

5. *Fine* hair is _____ (adj).
   a) thick   b) delicate   c) coarse

6. *Spun gold* means _____ (n).
   a) threads of gold   b) valuable   c) jewelry

7. *Braids* are _____ (n).
   a) ribbons   b) hats   c) hair twisted in threes

8. The *scalp* is the skin of the_____ (n).
   a) face   b) neck   c) head

Clue 3

The father is filled with *terror* at the sight of the witch. Even though he promises her the child, when Rapunzel is born, the parents beg the witch not to take their baby, but *to no avail*.

9. *Terror* is _____ (n).
   a) peace   b) destruction   c) fear

10. *To no avail* means _____ (idiom).
    a) successfully   b) unsuccessfully   c) inexpensively

Clue 4

Why does the witch suddenly decide to lock Rapunzel in a tower when she reaches *adolescence?* According to the story, Rapunzel lives outside of the tower in her childhood.

11. *Adolescence* is _____ (n).
    a) school   b) a road   c) teenage years

Clue 5

The witch is so angry that she wants both Rapunzel and the prince to suffer, and she is very *vicious.*

12. *Vicious* means _____ (adj).
    a) unhappy   b) mean   c) violent

Clue 6

The prince *asks* Rapunzel *for her hand.*

13. *Ask for someone's hand* means _____ (idiom).
    a) to want to get married   b) to want some help   c) to ask for money

Clue 7

Rapunzel feels such love for the prince that, when her tears fall into his eyes, her tears *restore* his sight.

14. *Restore* means _____ (v).
    a) to remove   b) to return   c) to shop

Questions for Discussion

First, reread the story carefully looking for the deeper meanings and reviewing the vocabulary. Then in groups of four discuss the following questions with your classmates. Be sure to tell what your native culture is.
1. What was your favorite sentence in this story and why?
2. Was Rapunzel ungrateful to the witch when she so quickly decided to marry the prince? What would a good daughter choose in your culture?
3. Was the prince's punishment justified?

Putting All the Pieces Together

Look at the puzzles on page 18 and page 23. Find the pieces that fit this story and discuss what cultural values this folktale teaches American children.

Double-checking the Vocabulary

Match the definitions with the words.

a. unsuccessfully
b. to propose marriage
c. with no color
d. fantastic, glorious, wonderful
e. to desire intensely
f. teenage years
g. parted in three and woven together
h. to be temptingly delicious
i. the skin that covers the head and holds the hair
j. to give back
k. strong fear
l. extremely cruel and dangerous

1. braids
2. splendid
3. pale
4. crave
5. to make a mouth water
6. terror
7. to no avail
8. adolescence
9. to ask for one's hand
10. scalp
11. vicious
12. restore

Writing

Think, *in English*, about the most similar story in your culture. Then, using the vocabulary words, write it, *in English*, in correct American form and as briefly as possible.

Speaking

Now, tell your story.

The Frog Prince

Reading Readiness

A. With a partner look at this cartoon. Describe what you see. Try to guess the names of the characters in the story and what the story will be about.

B. Look at these questions and share your ideas with the class.
1. Have you ever touched a frog? Describe what it felt like.
2. When can a promise be broken and when should it be kept?

Background Notes

This is a story collected by the Brothers Grimm in Germany in 1823. However, the theme—that a witch changes a handsome man (or woman) into something ugly and he (she) can only be changed back by the test of true love—had been common in England since the Middle Ages.

Reading Selection

Now read this story once, as quickly as possible, for the general idea. Try to guess the meanings of the words you don't understand by the context. You can underline the words you don't know, but don't stop reading.

In olden times, when people could have all that they wished for at once, there lived a king who had many beautiful daughters, but the youngest was the most beautiful by far. She had a favorite toy, which was a little golden ball, and she used to amuse herself by throwing it up high in the air, watching it sparkle in the sun, and then catching it. One day she was playing near a well and she threw the golden ball too far. Alas, it landed in the deep blue well. The princess began to weep and lament, when suddenly she heard a strange voice. "Oh, king's daughter, why are you weeping?" To her surprise, she saw a large green frog stretching his ugly head out of the water. It was he who spoke. "Oh, I have lost my favorite ball," she cried. "I can get it for you. What will you give me if I do?" the frog croaked. "Oh, I will give my gold and my pearls," said the princess. "I care not for your jewels, dear princess, but if you promise to love me and let me be your husband and sit with you at the table, drink from your golden cup, eat from your plate, and sleep with you in your nice little bed, I will dive down into the well and bring up your pretty golden ball." The princess was shocked at this and felt he was talking nonsense. Besides, he could never catch her when she ran home, so she promised that she would be his wife. The frog immediately dove to the bottom of the well, got the ball, and brought it to the princess in his mouth. She was full of joy and ran away as fast as she could. "Wait, wait," cried the frog. "Don't forget your promise." But the princess quickly forgot as she played with her ball.

The next night, as the princess and the royal family were eating dinner, they heard a strange noise on the marble stairs, splish, splash, splish, splash. Then there was a knock on the door. "Lovely princess, open the door for me." She went to open the door, and when she saw that ugly frog, she quickly slammed the door and ran back to the table. "My daughter, who is at the door and why are you so frightened?" asked her father, the king. "Is it some giant coming to carry you away?"

"Oh, no, my father. It is a great ugly frog!"

"A frog! And what would he want with you?"

And so the princess told her father how the frog had saved her ball. Just then, there was a second knock, and a voice cried,

> Open the door my darling, my heart,
> Open the door, my own dear thing,
> And remember the words that you and I spoke
> Down in the garden by the wellspring.

"My daughter, a promise is a promise, and it must be kept. Go and open the door," said the king. The frog hopped into the room and said,

Take me on your knee, my darling,
Take me on your knee, my own sweet thing,
And remember the words that you and I spoke
Down in the garden by the wellspring.

With a look of disgust, she did as she was told.

"And now, dear princess, lift me to the table so I may share your dinner." The princess begged her father, "Please don't make me!" but her father only said, "My daughter, a promise is a promise, and it must be kept." So she lifted the ugly frog to the table.

"Now put your plate closer to me that I may eat out of it," said the frog. The princess did as she was told, but everyone saw how she disliked doing it.

"Now let me drink out of your golden cup."

And then the frog said, "I have eaten and drunk enough and now I am tired. Carry me to your little bedroom." And the princess carried him by two fingers, holding him quite far from her body, and put him on her pillow. She was weeping, for she was really afraid of the cold frog. And you can be sure she slept close to the wall all night. When dawn came, the frog hopped out of bed and down the stairs, and he was gone. The princess was greatly relieved, for she thought that was the end of him. But that night at dinner she heard splish, splash, splish, splash on the marble stairs, and again she had to share her dinner and her bed with the frog. The third night the frog said, "You must kiss me on the lips, dear princess, or I shall tell your father." She was extremely frightened but knew that she had no choice. A promise is a promise, and it must be kept. She closed her eyes tightly and expected to feel wet, clammy lips, but instead the lips were warm and lovely. Surprised, the princess opened her eyes, and what did she see but a handsome prince! He told her that he had been bewitched by a wicked witch and forced to live in the well as a frog until a princess would come and release him. He asked for her hand and took her to his kingdom, where they were married and lived happily ever after.

Checking Your Comprehension

Answer these questions in class.

1. How does the princess meet the frog?
2. Why does the king make the princess obey the frog?
3. How was the prince changed into a frog?

Be a Vocabulary Detective

Working in pairs, look for hints and guess
the vocabulary from the context clues. Then
fill in the blanks with the correct answers.

Clue 1

Think about frogs. The handsome prince has
been turned into a frog. He *croaks* like a frog.
He feels cold and *clammy* like a frog. When
he climbs up the stairs of the palace, they
hear the sound of *splish, splash, splish, splash.*

1. *Croak* means_____ (v).
   a) to sing   b) to talk   c) to make a rough sound

2. *Clammy* means _____ (adj).
   a) soft   b) wet   c) dry

3. *Splish, splash* is a sound of_____ (n).
   a) wind   b) bells   c) water

Clue 2

The princess has a ball made out of gold. Playing with the ball *amuses* the
princess. When the ball is in the air, it *sparkles* in the sunlight.

4. *Amuse* means_____ (v).
   a) to please   b) to bore   c) to excite

5. *Sparkle* means_____ (v).
   a) to make noise   b) to shine   c) to darken

Clue 3

The ball is at the bottom of the well and the frog offers to *dive* deep into the well to get it.

6. *Dive* means _____ (v).
    a) to fly   b) to go deep down   c) to walk

Clue 4

The princess thinks that the ugly frog is talking *nonsense* when he asks her to be his bride. She is *shocked* to think that the frog would ask her to marry him, and she feels deep *disgust* when she looks at him.

7. *Nonsense* means _____ (n).
    a) something absurd   b) nothing   c) something loud

8. *Shocked* means _____ (adj).
    a) happy   b) greatly surprised   c) frightened

9. *Disgust* means _____ (n).
    a) delight   b) strong dislike   c) fear

Clue 5

The frog climbs up the white *marble* steps of the palace.
10. *Marble* is _____ (n).
    a) wood   b) stone   c) plastic

Clue 6

The princess spends a horrible night with the frog on her pillow, and when he leaves the next morning she feels *relieved*.

11. To feel *relieved* means _____ (adj).
    a) to feel relaxed   b) to feel confused   c) to feel lonely

Clue 7

The prince had been *bewitched* and turned into a frog by a wicked witch.

12. To be *bewitched* means _____ (adj).
    a) to be injured   b) to be kidnapped   c) to be put under a spell

Questions for Discussion

First, reread the story carefully looking for the deeper meanings and reviewing the vocabulary. Then in groups of four discuss the following questions with your classmates. Be sure to tell what your native culture is.

1. What was your favorite sentence in this story and why?
2. Did you think the king was fair to his daughter?
3. Do you think the princess acted properly?

Putting All the Pieces Together

Look at the puzzles on page 18 and page 23. Find the pieces that fit this story and discuss what cultural values this folktale teaches American children.

Double-checking the Vocabulary

Look at the definitions and cross out the words in the list that match. Then, looking at the words that remain, read from left to right, top to bottom, and find the answer to the question, "Why did the frog want to kiss the princess?"

a. a strong feeling of dislike
b. a hard, beautiful stone used for buildings and statues
c. to jump headfirst into the water
d. feeling unpleasant or angry surprise
e. to spend time in a pleasant way
f. having no meaning, absurd
g. a sound of water hitting the ground
h. to put under a magical spell
i. to shine light with small flashes
j. to speak with a rough, deep voice
k. a feeling of comfort because of the ending of fear or pain
l. unpleasantly sticky, damp, and cold

amuse	there	sparkle	croak
clammy	dive	bewitch	was
disgust	a	shock	fly
sitting	on	relief	marble
her	splish, splash	nonsense	lip

Writing

Think, *in English*, about the most similar story in your culture. Then, using the vocabulary words, write it, *in English*, in correct American form and as briefly as possible.

Speaking

Now, tell your story.

Sleeping Beauty

Reading Readiness

A. With a partner look at this advertisement. Describe what you see. Try to guess the names of the characters in the story and what the story will be about.

B. Look at these questions and share your ideas with the class.
   1. If you know that something very bad will happen, is there any way you can reverse it?
   2. Do you have any stories in your culture about a magic kiss?

Background Notes

This is from an old story of the 1300s told in France and Italy in which a beautiful young princess is threatened by a terrible spell. Nothing her parents can do will protect her. Only the kiss of love from a handsome prince can help, but he takes a very long time to come. This version was first written by Charles Perrault in France in 1697 and translated into English in 1765. It was made into an animated film by Walt Disney in 1959. You might want to watch the video after you read the story.

Reading Selection

Now read this story once, as quickly as possible, for the general idea. Try to guess the meanings of the words you don't understand by the context. You can underline the words you don't know, but don't stop reading.

Once upon a time there lived a good king and queen. They loved each other very much, and their people loved them. They had all the riches in the world and lacked only one thing to be happy. They had no children. At last the queen had a child, and what a beautiful little daughter she was! Everyone in the palace rejoiced, and the good king and queen planned a great celebration of thanksgiving. They invited all the fairies in the land, seven fairies in all, and seated them at a table that was set with special silverware. Each fairy received a beautiful fork, knife, and spoon, made of gold, diamonds, and rubies. Suddenly a very old and ugly fairy appeared. "And why was I not invited?" she screamed. No one had seen or heard of her for over fifty years and they had thought she was dead or enchanted. They tried to give her a gift as well, but there were no more forks, knives, or spoons made of gold, diamonds, and rubies in the castle.

After dinner all the fairies went to present their gifts to the new princess. The first fairy gave the princess beauty, the second gave her wit, the third gave her grace, the fourth gave her talent in dance, the fifth said that she would sing like a bird, the sixth said that she would play all kinds of music. Then the old fairy came very close to the cradle, stooped over, and shaking with anger said, "You may well have all those gifts, but they will do you no good, for I shall give you the gift of Death! You shall prick your finger on a spindle and die." With that, the old fairy vanished in a cloud of smoke. Everyone started to weep and wail, but the seventh fairy came forward and said, "I cannot undo the wicked curse of the old fairy, but I can add to it. Yes, the princess will prick her finger on a spindle, but she will not die. She will fall into a deep sleep for one hundred years, but then a king's son will come and awaken her."

The king immediately banished all spindles and any form of needles or sewing equipment from the kingdom and threatened the death sentence to anyone who would hide one in his or her house.

The princess grew, and everyone could see the gifts the fairies had given her. She was beautiful, talented, and bright. Her parents had never told her the story of the curse, and they thought of it seldom, as one remembers a bad dream.

One day, when the princess was sixteen, she was wandering around the castle and found a door that she had never seen before. She opened it and found a dark, narrow staircase leading to the tower. At the top of the stairs was a door. When she opened it she found an old woman spinning on a spindle. The princess was very interested, for she had never seen a spindle before. The old woman taught her how to spin and gave the princess a small spindle to practice with. When the princess went back to her room, she took out the spindle to practice spinning, pricked her finger, and immediately fell into a deep sleep. Her maid began to wail, and the king and queen came running. They realized that the curse had come true. As they placed the princess on her bed, the seventh fairy heard the lamenting and weeping and put a spell on the entire palace. Suddenly everyone fell asleep: the cooks stirring the soup in the kitchen, the baker baking bread, the cat on the chair, the birds in the cage, the mice in the walls, the horses in the stable. The entire palace was in a deep sleep, and a large forest of thornbushes immediately grew around the castle. For one hundred years young princes who had heard the tale of the Sleeping Beauty would try to cut through the thornbushes to get into the castle, but it was impossible, and no one ever got through.

Exactly one hundred years later, a young prince from a neighboring kingdom was hunting in the woods when he came upon the forest of thornbushes. As he touched them with his sword, they melted away, and he followed a path to the door of the castle. Entering, he saw an incredible sight. People and animals were asleep everywhere. They were wearing clothes quite out of style, but they all looked young and healthy. The baker was asleep at the oven door. The king sat on his throne, snoring. The cook stood at the stove with her spoon in the soup. In a bed chamber he found the loveliest young woman he had ever seen, asleep on her bed. He bent over her and kissed her tenderly on the lips. With that kiss, she opened her eyes, and the spell was broken. The king and queen, the courtiers, the workers, the animals all awoke and immediately realized that the curse had been lifted. Oh, what a great feasting there was! The prince asked for the princess's hand in marriage, and they rode away to his castle and lived happily ever after.

Checking Your Comprehension

Answer these questions in class.
1. Why does the old fairy curse the princess?
2. What is the curse?
3. Who do you think the old woman in the tower is?
4. What happens to the thornbushes at the end of the story? Why?

Be a Vocabulary Detective

Working in pairs, look for hints and guess the vocabulary from the context clues. Then fill in the blanks with the correct answers.

Clue 1

The good king and queen had everything except that they *lacked* a child, and this made them very sad.

1. *Lack* means _____ (v).
    a) to have   b) to want   c) to not have

Clue 2

The princess was given many wonderful gifts by the fairies. Everyone enjoyed talking to the princess because she was given the gift of *wit*. And they enjoyed watching her walk, sing, and dance because she had the gift of *grace*.

2. *Wit* means_____ (n).
    a) beauty   b) kindness   c) cleverness

3. *Grace* means_____ (n).
    a) gentleness   b) laughter   c) fineness in movement

Clue 3

The old fairy was very angry because she was not given a beautiful gift of a fork, knife, and spoon made of gold, diamonds, and red *rubies*. She went to the *cradle* where the baby princess was sleeping, *stooped over* the cradle, and *cast an evil spell* over the princess. Then the old fairy *vanished*. Years later, the curse came true. The princess *pricked* her finger on a spindle.

4. A *ruby* is _____ (n).
    a) wood   b) a precious stone   c) plastic

5. A *cradle* is_____ (n).
    a) a chair   b) a small bed   c) a table

6. *Stoop over* means _____ (v).
   a) to bend   b) to jump   c) to dance

7. *Cast a spell* means _____ (v).
   a) to talk   b) to bewitch   c) to laugh

8. *Vanish* means _____ (v).
   a) to disappear   b) to dance   c) to sing

9. *Prick* means _____ (v).
   a) to hit   b) to stick   c) to itch

Clue 4

The seventh fairy couldn't *undo* the spell, but she could change the ending. The king *banished* all sewing equipment from his kingdom.

10. *Undo* means _____ (v).
    a) to remove   b) to add to   c) to change

11. *Banish* means _____ (v).
    a) to allow   b) to not allow   c) to sell

Clue 5

Everyone was so sad when the curse came true, that they all began to *wail*.

12. *Wail* means _____ (v).
    a) to cry loudly   b) to laugh   c) to sigh

Clue 6

After one hundred years, when the king's son saw the forest of thornbushes, he touched them with his sword and they just *melted* away in front of him.

13. *Melt away* means _____ (v).
    a) to grow thick   b) to catch on fire   c) to disappear

Questions for Discussion

First, reread the story carefully looking for the deeper meanings and reviewing the vocabulary. Then in groups of four discuss the following questions with your classmates. Be sure to tell what your native culture is.

1. What was your favorite sentence in this story and why?
2. Do you think the princess (and the king and queen) deserved the punishment they received? (Did the punishment fit the crime?)
3. Why did the seventh fairy put the whole castle to sleep?

Putting All the Pieces Together

Look at the puzzles on page 18 and page 23. Find the pieces that fit this story and discuss what cultural values this folktale teaches American children.

Double-checking the Vocabulary

Fill in the crossword with the following vocabulary words: cast a spell, ruby, wit, grace, lack, cradle, prick, vanish, stoop over, wail, undo, banish, melt away. You will also need the word *male*.

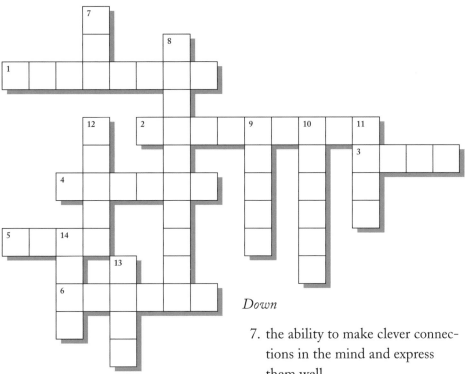

Down

7. the ability to make clever connections in the mind and express them well
8. to cause a condition by a magical power (three words)
9. to make a very small hole in the skin with a sharp object
10. to disappear quickly without a trace
11. a deep red precious stone
12. fineness in movement, form, and behavior
13. to cry loudly from deep sorrow
14. to not have

Across

1. to disappear as if having been dissolved (two words)
2. to bend over (two words)
3. to remove the effects of something
4. to send away
5. opposite of female
6. small bed for an infant

Writing

Think, *in English*, about the most similar story in your culture. Then, using the vocabulary words, write it, *in English*, in correct American form and as briefly as possible.

Speaking

Now, tell your story.

Chapter 7

Hard Work Pays Off

> Life grants nothing to us mortals without hard work.
> —Horace, 65-8 B.C.

> 'Tis a lesson, you should heed,
> Try, try again.
> If at first you don't succeed,
> Try, try again.
> —William Edward Hickson, 1803-70

The Three Little Pigs

Reading Readiness

A. With a partner look at this advertisement. Describe what you see. Try to guess the names of the characters in the story and what the story will be about.

MIRACLE BRICK Looks like Brick, Feels Like Brick, Stronger than Brick, Guaranteed Earthquake Safe, Tornado Safe – No Huffing or Puffing Could Ever Blow It Down.

A New Polyurethene Building Material, Pat. Pend.

B. Look at these questions and share your ideas with the class.

1. In this story three little pigs live with their mother. Whom do they live with in your culture—with their mother or their father, or do just the three brothers live together?

2. In this story the mother gives advice to her children. List three different pieces of advice a good mother would give to her children in your culture.

Background Notes

This folktale is very old and is popular in French and English speaking countries. It's about three pigs who are brothers. They leave their home and make houses out of straw and twigs and brick. You probably have a similar story in your culture. You might not have a story about pigs, but you might have a similar story about three little sheep, oxen, goats, or rabbits.

Reading Selection

Now read this story once, as quickly as possible, for the general idea. Try to guess the meanings of the words you don't understand by the context. You can underline the words you don't know, but don't stop reading.

Once there were three little pigs who lived with their mother in a little house at the edge of a deep woods.

The little pigs grew, as piglets do. One day their mother said, "This house is too small for all of us. It is time for you piglets to go out into the world and make homes for yourselves."

The three little pigs said good-bye to their mother and went out into the world to make homes for themselves.

When they came to a crossroads, the first little pig sat down with a sigh. "I will wait right here," he said, "and see what comes along."

The second little pig took the path that led into the deep woods. And the third little pig took the road toward town.

As the first little pig waited at the crossroads, along came a man with a load of straw.

"Ah," said the first little pig to himself. "It would be easy to build a house with straw."

So he said to the man, "Please, sir, give me some straw to build a house."

The man did. And one, two, three—the first little pig built himself a flimsy little house of straw.

But the little pig did not know that a wolf had been watching him from deep in the woods.

No sooner had the little pig moved into his house of straw than along came the hungry wolf.

"Little pig, little pig, let me come in," he said.

"No, by the hair of my chinny, chin, chin, I will not let you in," said the first little pig.

"Then I'll huff and I'll puff and I'll blow your house in," said the wolf. He took a deep breath. And he huffed and he puffed and he blew the house in. And that was the end of the first little pig.

The second little pig walked down the path that led into the deep woods. Soon he met a man with a bundle of twigs.

"Ah," said the second little pig to himself. "It would be easy to build a house with twigs."

So he said to the man, "Please, sir, give me some twigs to build a house."

The man did. And one, two, three—the second little pig built himself a flimsy little house of twigs.

But the little pig did not know that the wolf had been watching him from deep in the woods.

No sooner had the little pig moved into his house of twigs than the hungry wolf came knocking at his door.

"Little pig, little pig, let me come in," said the wolf.

"No, by the hair of my chinny, chin, chin, I will not let you in," said the little pig.

"Then I'll huff and I'll puff and I'll blow your house in," said the wolf.

He took a deep, deep breath. And he huffed and he puffed and he huffed and he puffed and he blew the house in. And that was the end of the second little pig.

The third little pig walked down the road toward town until he met a man with a load of bricks.

"H'm," said the little pig to himself. "Those bricks would make a sturdy little house."

So he said to the man, "Please, sir, give me some of those bricks to build a house."

The man gave him some bricks. And the third little pig set to work. It was not easy. But he kept at it. And before long his house was built. By this time the wolf was hungry again. He came along just as the little pig had moved into his new house of brick.

"Little pig, little pig, let me come in," he said.

"No, by the hair of my chinny, chin, chin, I will not let you in," said the little pig.

"Then I'll huff and I'll puff and I'll blow your house in," said the wolf.

He took a deep, deep breath. And he huffed and he puffed and he puffed and he huffed, but he could not blow down that little brick house.

This made the wolf very angry. He took a run and a jump and landed on the roof. He planned to come down the chimney and eat up the third little pig.

But the little pig heard him, and he knew just what to do. He filled a big kettle with water, put it on the fire to boil, and sat down to wait for the wolf.

Down came the wolf into the kettle of water, and that was the end of him.

As for the little pig, he lived happily on in his sturdy little house of brick.

Checking Your Comprehension

Answer these questions in class.
1. What happened to the first and second little pigs? Did that surprise you?
2. Why did the third little pig survive?
3. Who killed the wolf?

Be a Vocabulary Detective

Working in pairs, look for hints and guess the vocabulary from the context clues. Then fill in the blanks with the correct answers.

Clue 1

The little *piglets* feel safe in their house at the *edge* of a *deep woods*. But they have to go into the wide world because the house is *too* small.

1. A *piglet* is _____ (n).
    a) a brother   b) a small pig   c) something to eat

2. *Edge* means _____ (n).
    a) the middle   b) the border   c) a sidewalk

3. *Deep woods* means _____ (n).
    a) lumber   b) a valley   c) a forest

4. *Too* means _____ (adv).
    a) extremely in a negative way   b) extremely in a positive way   c) also

Clue 2

The pigs come to a *crossroads* and have to make a decision about where they will go in their lives. The first little pig decides to let things happen to him, and he sits down and *sighs*. The second little pig chooses the *path* that leads into the dark woods.

5. A *crossroads* is _____ (n).
    a) a freeway   b) an intersection   c) a restaurant

6. *Sigh* means _____ (v).
    a) to breathe out air in frustration   b) to make music   c) to rest

7. A *path* is _____ (n).
    a) the opposite of fail   b) a popular street   c) a very small road

Clue 3

The first and second little pigs are so lazy that they build *flimsy* houses out of straw and twigs, but the third little pig builds a *sturdy* house out of bricks.

8. *Flimsy* means _____ (adj).
    a) strong   b) weak   c) flammable

9. *Sturdy* means _____ (adj).
    a) strong   b) weak   c) flammable

Clue 4

The wolf knocks on the doors of the little pigs' houses, but the little pigs promise by the *hairs of their chinny, chin, chins* that they will not open the doors. Then the wolf *huffs and puffs* trying to blow the houses down.

10. By the *hair of my chinny, chin, chin* is a nonsense rhyme, but it comes from the tradition of telling the truth by swearing by your (or your father's) _____ (n).

    a) honor   b) soul   c) beard

11. *Huff and puff* means _____ (v).
    a) to breathe in and out strongly   b) to laugh and cry at the same time
    c) to smoke a pipe

Clue 5

The third little pig knows that the wolf is coming down the chimney (and it definitely is not Santa Claus), so he fills a large *kettle* of water and puts it on the fire to boil.

12. A *kettle* is _____ (n).
    a) a pot   b) a brick   c) a stove

Questions for Discussion

First, reread the story carefully looking for the deeper meanings and reviewing the vocabulary. Then in groups of four discuss the following questions with your classmates. Be sure to tell what your native culture is.
1. What was your favorite sentence in this story and why?
2. Do you think it makes a difference if there is a mother in the story or not?
3. Do you think it makes a difference if the pigs get eaten or if they escape to safety to their brothers' houses? Explain your answer.
4. Explain what relationship the cartoon on the following page has to the story.

"Well, it could be worse. We could be like these trees and our kids would never move away from home."

Putting All the Pieces Together

Look at the puzzles on page 18 and page 23. Find the pieces that fit this story and discuss what cultural values this folktale teaches American children.

Double-checking the Vocabulary

Look at the definitions and cross out the words in the list that match. Then, looking at the words that remain, read from left to right, top to bottom, and find the answer to the question, "What did the third little pig cook for dinner?"

a. of poor quality, badly made
b. an intersection
c. a small infrequently traveled road
d. a beard
e. an emphasis word that is frequently negative
f. the end of something, border
g. to breathe in and out with great effort
h. a young pig
i. strong, well-made
j. to breathe out air because of sadness or frustration
k. a utensil for boiling liquid

crossroads	he	sturdy
made	flimsy	piglet
huff and puff	wolf	path
kettle	soup	edge
too	sigh	the hair of my chinny, chin, chin

Writing

Think, *in English*, about the most similar story in your culture. Then, using the vocabulary words, write it, *in English*, in correct American form and as briefly as possible.

Speaking

Now, tell your story.

Hansel and Gretel

Reading Readiness

A. With a partner look at this advertisement. Describe what you see. Try to guess the names of the characters in the story and what the story will be about.

Gretel's Gingerbread House Mix

Just Add Water and Follow Directions – It's like Magic! Your Children Will Nibble, Nibble on This House

Batter, Sugar Frosting, Gum Drops, All Included

B. Look at the questions and share your ideas with the class.
1. Were you ever lost when you were a little child? Do you remember the feeling?
2. Have you ever been in a dangerous situation in which you used your common sense to escape the danger? Describe this situation.

Background Notes

This story about a brother and sister who love each other and protect one another from an evil stepmother and a weak father was collected by the Brothers Grimm. The story has a common theme in folktales. It deals with universal fears that children have: fear of separation from the parents and fear of being eaten by some terrible monster. This particular story is very famous and was made into a German opera, written in 1893, by Englebert Humperdinck.

Reading Selection

Now read this story once, as quickly as possible, for the general idea. Try to guess the meanings of the words you don't understand by the context. You can underline the words you don't know, but don't stop reading.

Close to a large forest there lived a woodcutter with his wife and two children. The boy was called Hansel and the girl Gretel. They were always very poor and had very little to live on. Suddenly there was a famine in the land. The woodcutter could no longer earn his daily bread.

One night, when he lay in bed worrying over his troubles, he sighed and said to his wife, "What is to become of us? How are we to feed our poor children when we have nothing for ourselves?"

"I'll tell you what, husband," answered the woman (who was the children's stepmother). "Tomorrow morning we will take the children out into the thickest part of the forest. We will light a fire and give each of them a piece of bread. Then we will go to our work and leave them alone. They won't be able to find their way back, and so we will be rid of them."

"Nay, wife," said the man, "we won't do that. I could never find it in my heart to leave my children alone in the forest. Wild animals would soon tear them to pieces."

"What a fool you are!" said the wife. "Then we must all four die of hunger." She gave him no peace until he consented. "But I am so sorry for my poor children all the same," said the man.

The two children could not go to sleep for hunger either, and they heard what their stepmother said to their father.

Gretel wept bitterly and said, "All is over with us now."

"Be quiet, Gretel," said Hansel. "Don't cry. I will find some way out of it."

When the parents had gone to sleep, Hansel got up, put on his little coat, opened the door, and slipped out. The moon was shining brightly, and the white pebbles round the house shone like new pennies. Hansel bent down and put as many pebbles in his pockets as they would hold.

Then he went back to Gretel and said, "Take comfort, little sister, and go to sleep." And he went to bed again.

At dawn, the stepmother came and said, "Get up, you lazybones! We are going into the forest to find wood."

Then she gave them each a piece of bread and said, "Here is something for your dinner, but don't eat it before then, for you'll get no more."

Gretel put the bread in her bag, for Hansel had the stones in his pockets, and they all started to the forest. When they had gone a little way, Hansel stopped and looked back at the house. He did the same thing again and again.

His father said, "Hansel what are you stopping to look at? You are wasting time."

"Oh, Father," said Hansel, "I am looking at my white cat. It is sitting on the roof, wanting to say good-bye to me."

"Little fool, that's no cat! It's the morning sun shining on the chimney," said the stepmother.

But Hansel had not been looking at the cat. He had dropped a pebble on the ground each time he stopped.

When they reached the middle of the forest, their father said, "Now children, pick up some wood. I want to make a fire to warm you." Hansel and Gretel gathered the twigs together and soon made a huge pile. The pile was lighted, and when it blazed up the woman said, "Now lie down by the fire and rest yourselves while we go and cut wood. When we have finished we will come back to get you."

Hansel and Gretel sat by the fire, and when dinnertime came they each ate their little bit of bread. They thought that their father was still quite near because they could hear the sound of an ax. It was no ax, however, but a branch that the man had tied to a dead tree so that the branch blew backward and forward against the tree. Hansel and Gretel sat there so long that they got tired. Their eyes began to close, and they were soon fast asleep.

When they woke it was dark. Gretel began to cry, "How will we ever get out of the woods?"

But Hansel comforted her and said, "Wait a while till the moon rises, and then we can see our way."

When the full moon rose, Hansel took his little sister's hand and they walked on, guided by the pebbles, which glittered like newly coined money. They walked the whole night, and at daybreak they were back at their father's house.

They knocked at the door, and when their stepmother opened it she said, "You bad children, why did you sleep so long in the woods? We thought you had run away."

But their father was delighted, for he felt very bad that he had left them behind alone.

Not long afterward their poverty returned, and one night the children heard their stepmother say to their father, "We have eaten up everything but half a loaf and then we will have no more. The children must go away! We will take them farther into the forest so that they won't be able to find their way back. There is nothing else to be done."

The man said, "No, we had better share our last crust with the children."

But the stepmother would not listen to a word he said. She only scolded and argued with him. Anyone who once says A must also say B, and as the father had given in the first time, he had to do so the second time. The children were wide awake and heard everything that was said.

When the old people went to sleep Hansel again got up, planning to get more pebbles. But the stepmother had locked the door, and he couldn't get out. He comforted his little sister and said, "Don't cry, Gretel. Go to sleep."

In the early morning the stepmother woke the children. She gave them each a piece of bread, smaller than last time. On the way to the forest Hansel crumbled it up in his pocket and stopped every now and then to throw a crumb on the ground.

"Hansel, what are you stopping to look at?" asked his father.

"I am looking at my dove, which is sitting on the roof and wants to say good-bye to me," answered Hansel.

"Little fool, that's no dove! It's the morning sun shining on the chimney," said the stepmother.

Nevertheless Hansel dropped the crumbs on the ground every time he stopped. The stepmother led the children far into the forest to a place where they had never been before.

Again they made a big fire, and the stepmother said, "Stay where you are, children, and when you are tired lie down by the fire and rest yourselves while we go and cut wood. When we have finished we will come back to get you."

When dinnertime came Gretel shared her bread with Hansel, for he had crumbled his on the road. Their eyes began to close, and they were soon fast asleep.

When they woke it was dark. Gretel began to cry, "How will we ever get out of the woods?"

But Hansel comforted her and said, "Wait a while till the moon rises and then we will see the bread crumbs that I scattered to help us find our way home."

When the moon rose, Hansel took his little sister's hand and they walked on, but they found no bread crumbs, for all the birds in the forest had picked them up and eaten them.

Hansel said to Gretel, "We shall soon find the way." But they could not find it. They walked the whole night and all the next day from morning till night, but they could not get out of the woods.

They were very hungry, and they could find nothing to eat but a few berries. They were so tired that their legs would not carry them any farther and they lay down under a tree and went to sleep.

When they woke in the morning, it was the third day since they had left their father's house. They started to walk again, but they only got deeper and deeper into the woods. If no help came they would die.

At midday they saw a beautiful snow-white bird sitting on a tree. It sang so beautifully that they stood still to listen to it. When it stopped, it fluttered its wings and flew around them. They followed it till they came to a little house. The bird settled down on the roof of the house.

The children stood hand in hand and stared at the house in wonder. "It's the loveliest house I ever saw," gasped Gretel, "and it looks good enough to eat!"

Hansel touched the house and cried, "Gretel, it *is* good enough to eat!" For the little house was made of gingerbread and roofed with cake. The windows were made of transparent sugar and trimmed with cookies and candies. Nothing could have pleased the children better, and they began eating right away. Hansel plucked a cookie from the roof and took a big bite out of it. Gretel munched big pieces of sugar that she had broken from the window.

A gentle voice called out from within, "Nibbling, nibbling like a mouse, who's that nibbling at my house?" And the children answered, "It's only a breeze, blowing down from the trees." And they went on eating without disturbing themselves. All at once the door opened, and an old, old woman came limping out on a crutch. Hansel and Gretel were so frightened that they dropped the goodies they held in their hands. The old woman was very ugly. Her sharp nose bent down to meet her hairy chin. Her face, all folds and wrinkles, looked like an old dried apple. She had only three teeth, two above and one below, all very long and yellow.

The old woman only shook her head and said, "Ah, dear children, who brought you here? Come in and stay with me. You will come to no harm."

She took them into her little house. A nice dinner was put before them—pancakes and sugar, milk, apples, and nuts. After this she showed them two white beds into which they climbed and felt as if they were in heaven.

But though the old woman appeared to be friendly, she was really a wicked old witch who was on the watch for children, and she had built the gingerbread house on purpose to lead them to her. Whenever she could get a child into her house she ate the child and considered it a grand feast. Witches have red eyes and can't see very well, but oh! how they can smell with their long noses! "Mmm, mmm, mmm!" she said. "They will be a juicy dinner."

Early the next morning she seized Hansel out of bed, dragged him into the backyard, and locked him in a chicken coop. Hansel screamed and cried, but it did him no good.

Then she went to Gretel and shook her till she woke and cried, "Get up, little lazybones! Get some water and cook something nice for your brother. He is in the chicken coop and has to be fattened. When he is nice and fat, I will eat him."

Gretel began to cry bitterly, but it was no use. She had to obey the witch's orders. The best food was cooked for poor Hansel, but Gretel got only the crumbs.

Every day the old woman went to the chicken coop and said, "Hansel, put your finger out for me to feel how fat you are." Hansel put out a chicken bone, and the old witch, whose eyes were too dim to see, thought that it was his finger. She was very astonished that he was not getting fat.

After four weeks Hansel was still thin. The witch became impatient and could wait no longer.

"Now then, Gretel," she cried, "hurry along and get some water. Fat or thin, I will kill Hansel and eat him."

Oh, how his poor little sister cried! As she carried the water the tears streamed down her cheeks. She begged and pleaded, but the old woman said, "You may spare your lamentations! They will do no good."

Gretel had to go out to fill the kettle with water, and she had to build a fire and hang the kettle over it.

"We will bake bread first," said the old witch. "I have heated the oven." She pushed poor Gretel toward the oven and said in a sweet voice, "Do you think it's hot enough for the bread, Gretel dear? Just stick your head in and see; there's a good girl." She meant, when Gretel had looked in, to push her in and roast her. Gretel suspected this and she said, "Well, I really don't know how to go about it. Couldn't you first show me how?" "Stupid!" cried the witch. "It's easy enough."

She limped over and stuck her head into the oven. Gretel gave her a push and sent the witch right in. Then she closed the door and locked it. "Oh, oh!" screamed the witch. But Gretel ran as fast as she could to Hansel and left the old witch to bake and perish.

Hansel jumped out like a bird from a cage. How happy they were! They kissed each other and danced about for joy.

As they had nothing more to fear, they went into the witch's house, and in every corner they found chests full of pearls and precious stones.

"These are better than pebbles," said Hansel, as he filled his pockets.

Gretel said, "I must take something home with me too." And she filled her bag.

"But now we must go." said Hansel, "We must get out of this enchanted woods."

Before they had gone very far, they came to a lake. "We can't get across it. There are no stepping-stones and no bridge and no boats. But there is a swan." So the children said, "Float, swan, float, be our little boat." The swan took the children, one by one, to the other side, and, as they walked, the woods seemed to grow more and more familiar to them. At last they saw their father's house in the distance. They began to run, rushed inside, and threw their arms around their father's neck. "My treasures, my little treasures," he said with tears in his eyes.

"Oh! as to treasures, papa," said Hansel, "we'll show you some!" And he emptied his pockets and Gretel emptied her bag.

And the hard-hearted stepmother, where was she? Well, her husband had not been happy for a single moment since he deserted his children in the woods. That made her so angry that she packed her things in a large red handkerchief and ran away. She never came back, and Hansel and Gretel and their good father lived happily ever after.

Checking Your Comprehension

Answer these questions in class.
1. Why do the parents want to get rid of Hansel and Gretel?
2. Why do Hansel and Gretel get trapped by the witch?
3. How do they save themselves?

Be a Vocabulary Detective

Working in pairs, look for hints and guess the vocabulary from the context clues. Then fill in the blanks with the correct answers.

Clue 1

The woodcutter and his family are extremely poor. There is no food in the land because there is a *famine*. They will surely die, for all that is left to eat is a *crust* of bread.

1. A *famine* is _____ (n).
    a) a big dinner   b) a party   c) no food

2. A *crust* is_____ (n).
    a) the outside of the bread   b) a cracker   c) jelly

Clue 2

Hansel is very clever. He marks his way back to the house by dropping little markers from his pocket. He *scatters* some bright *pebbles* on the ground. He takes the bread and *crumbles* it. He drops the *crumbs* in the forest.

3. *Scatter* means _____ (v).
    a) to eat   b) to throw   c) to buy

4. A *pebble* is _____ (n).
    a) a mountain   b) a map   c) a small stone

5. *Crumble* means _____ (v).
    a) to repair   b) to buy   c) to make small

6. A *crumb* is _____ (n).
    a) a very small piece   b) a mark   c) a sign

Clue 3

Both the stepmother and the witch *scold* the children and say that they are *lazybones*. Gretel often cries *bitterly*.

7. *Scold* means _____ (v).
   a) to speak angrily   b) to compliment   c) to burn

8. *Lazybones* means _____ (n).
   a) skeleton   b) a person who doesn't work   c) some meat

9. *Bitterly* means_____ (adv).
   a) sadly   b) happily   c) loudly

Clue 4

The witch is very ugly and very old. She can't see well without a lot of light because her vision is very *dim*. She walks with a *limp* and needs to use a *crutch*.

10. *Dim* is _____ (adj).
    a) unclear   b) bright   c) blind

11. *Limp* means _____ (v).
    a) to hop   b) to walk unevenly   c) to fall

12. A *crutch* is _____ (n).
    a) a support   b) a chair   c) part of a car

Clue 5

The children find a marvelous house made out of sugar, cookies, and gingerbread. Not too sure if it is really made out of food, they begin to *nibble* at the house. When they realize that the house can be eaten, Gretel *munches* on the sugar from the windows.

13. *Nibble* means _____ (v).
    a) to take little bites   b) to cook   c) to knock

14. *Munch* means_____ (v).
    a) to eat   b) to drink   c) to climb

Questions for Discussion

First, reread the story carefully looking for the deeper meanings and reviewing the vocabulary. Then in groups of four discuss the following questions with your classmates. Be sure to tell what your native culture is.
1. What was your favorite sentence in this story and why?
2. What did you think about the father?
3. Who took better care of the other, Hansel or Gretel? Explain.

Putting All the Pieces Together

Look at the puzzles on page 18 and page 23. Find the pieces that fit this story and discuss what cultural values this folktale teaches American children.

Double-checking the Vocabulary

Look at the definitions and cross out the words in the list that match. Then, looking at the words that remain, read from left to right, top to bottom, and find the answer to the question, "Why should Hansel and Gretel *not* nibble at the gingerbread house?"

a. to speak in an angry way
b. the outside of a loaf of bread
c. to take very little bites
d. to walk unevenly
e. small stones
f. a person who won't do any work
g. with deep and angry sorrow
h. to spread in all directions
i. no food in the land/a time of starvation
j. extremely small pieces of bread or cookies
k. to break into very small pieces
l. a support
m. not bright
n. eat

famine	bitterly	they	lazybones	crust	were
scold	crumble	supposed	crumbs	to	scatter
be	munch	on	limp	a	pebbles
crutch	nonfat	dim	nibble	diet	

Writing

Think, *in English*, about the most similar story in your culture. Then, using the vocabulary words, write it, *in English*, in correct American form and as briefly as possible.

Speaking

Now, tell your story.

John Henry

Reading Readiness

A. With a partner look at this picture. Describe what you see. Try to guess the names of the characters in the story and what the story will be about.

B. Look at these questions and share your ideas with the class.
1. Do you think that there is anything worth dying for? Explain.
2. Which is superior, man or machine?

Background Notes

In the 1860s, the Chesapeake and Ohio Railroad Company wanted to put in railroad tracks in the state of West Virginia. They needed to make a train tunnel through the Allegheny Mountains. To accomplish this, they hired thousands of workers, called steel drivers, to hammer steel spikes into the solid rock. The spikes would make holes into which the steel drivers would put dynamite. The explosions would cut pieces out of the mountain. That was how they made tunnels in those days. In the 1870s an African-American steel driver named John Henry became very famous for his great strength. His story became an American hero tale, a work song, and a popular ballad. You might want to listen to the songs after you read this story.

Reading Selection

Now read this story once, as quickly as possible, for the general idea. Try to guess the meanings of the words you don't understand by the context. You can underline the words you don't know, but don't stop reading.

The night John Henry was born there was no moon. The sky was dark, and there was thunder and lightning. His mama and papa were real surprised when they saw their baby because he weighed forty-two pounds. He had a man's deep voice, a big smile, and he was born with a hammer in his hand. His mama said, "He looks just like my granddaddy who came from Africa." And his papa said, "He looks like he's brought his strength from Africa, too."

When John Henry was ten years old he started working for the Chesapeake and Ohio Railroad Company as a steel driver. Years later he fell in love with another steel driver, Lucy Ann, and they got married.

People who saw him said that John Henry could hold the hammer in his mouth with his hands tied behind him and hammer so hard that even the strongest steel drivers, hammering with both their hands, would be as far behind John Henry as the moon is behind the sun. John Henry would laugh and say, "I'm just a natural man."

The July of John Henry's thirty-fourth year was the hottest July in history. Many workers collapsed from heatstroke. John Henry would pick up their hammers and do their work for them. When they would thank him he would say, "A man ain't nothing but a man. He's just got to do his best."

August was even hotter. A new work crew came into town. They had a steam drill machine. "Our machine can drill holes faster than a dozen men working together," their boss said. John Henry said, "No, I can drill faster than a machine or I'll die with my hammer in my hand."

And so they had a contest. If John Henry won, he'd get $100. "That contest will be the death of you, John Henry. And if you die, your poor wife and child will never smile again," said Lucy Ann. But John Henry lifted his baby in the air and said, "Johnny, a man ain't nothing but a man. He's just got to do his best. Tomorrow I'll take my hammer in my hand and drive faster than any machine." They all laughed at John Henry. "No man can beat a machine, not until the rocks in that mountain turn to gold."

The next day at dawn the sun was hotter than ever before. The contest started at 6:30 A.M. John Henry started hammering with two hammers, one in each hand. That steam drill machine started drilling, and they both tunneled into the Big Bend Mountain. John Henry hammered so fast they had to throw water on the hammers to keep the iron from melting. They had to throw water to keep the sparks from starting a fire.

When the contest was over, the machine had drilled nine feet. John Henry had dug seven feet—but with each hand! So he won because he had drilled fourteen feet. But just at the end of the contest they heard a tremendous crash, and John Henry fell to the ground. He had hammered so fast and so hard that his ribs broke and his insides came out of his body. He hammered so fast that his heart broke.

Lucy Ann ran to him with some water. He smiled at her and said, "I beat that machine," and he died with his hammer in his hand.

All the people cried and came to his funeral. The epitaph on his gravestone reads, "Here lies a steel driving man." And some folks say that sometimes on a Monday morning, near the Big Bend Tunnel, you can still hear John Henry's hammer ring.

Checking Your Comprehension

Answer these questions in class.
1. What is John Henry's occupation?
2. What are the names of his wife and his child?
3. Why does John Henry accept the contest with the machine?
4. Why does John Henry die?

Be a Vocabulary Detective

Working in pairs, look for hints and guess the vocabulary from the context clues. Then fill in the blanks with the correct answers.

Clue 1

The Chesapeake and Ohio Railroad Company needed a *tunnel* in the mountain so that they could put in train *tracks*.

1. A *tunnel* is _____ (n).
   a) a bridge   b) a path   c) an underground passage

2. A *track* is _____ (n).
   a) a game   b) a large car   c) metal guides

Clue 2

In those days, the men had to *drill* holes in the mountain. They drilled the holes with *spikes*, which were made out of *steel*. They pounded the spikes into the mountain with *hammers*. Then they filled the holes with *dynamite*, and the explosions opened the mountain.

3. *Drill* means _____ (v).
   a) to make a repetitive action to make a hole   b) to test
   c) to go to the dentist

4. A *spike* is _____ (n).
   a) a thorn   b) a long, pointed object   c) a drink

5. *Steel* is _____ (n).
   a) a form of iron   b) a theft   c) plastic

6. A *hammer* is a tool to use with _____ (n).
   a) screws   b) nails   c) water

7. *Dynamite* is in _____ (n).
   a) food   b) money   c) bombs

Clue 3

The men were working in the hot sun, and they *collapsed* because they had *heatstroke*.

8. *Collapse* means _____ (v).
   a) to fall down   b) to jump up   c) to win a contest

9. *Heatstroke* is _____ (n).

   a) a heart attack   b) a fever   c) an illness from the sun

Clue 4

John Henry is not an educated man, and he speaks an informal English. He says, "A man *ain't* nothing but a man."

10. *Ain't* means _____ (nonstandard).

   a) am, is, or are not   B) does not   C) cannot

Clue 5

Lucy Ann writes, "Here lies a steel driving man," for his *epitaph*.

11. An *epitaph* is _____ (n).

   a) a stone   b) a final message   c) a funeral

Clue 6

After John Henry died they sang many famous *ballads* about him.

12. A *ballad* is _____ (n).

   a) a toy   b) a dance   c) a song

Questions for Discussion

First, reread the story carefully looking for the deeper meanings and reviewing the vocabulary. Then in groups of four discuss the following questions with your classmates. Be sure to tell what your native culture is.
1. What was your favorite sentence in this story and why?
2. In the world today, which is really the master, machines or human beings?
3. What did John Henry mean when he said he was "a natural man"?

Putting All the Pieces Together

Look at the puzzles on page 18 and page 23. Find the pieces that fit this story and discuss what cultural values this hero tale teaches American children.

Double-checking the Vocabulary

Match the definitions with the words.

a. a powerful explosive used in mining
b. a short story told in a poem often set to music
c. an underground passage, under a hill, water, mountain
d. a long, sharp, pointed piece of metal
e. an often life threatening condition caused by being in the sun too long; sunstroke
f. metal lines on which a train runs
g. a nonstandard form of English used to state a negative with the verb *to be*
h. a tool with a heavy head for driving nails, etc., into hard surfaces
i. a short description of a dead person, often written on the stone above the grave
j. a repetitive action to make a hole
k. to fall down or inward suddenly
l. a form of hard iron mixed with carbon or other metals

1. railroad tracks
2. tunnel
3. drilling
4. steel
5. spike
6. dynamite
7. hammer
8. ballad
9. collapse
10. heatstroke
11. ain't
12. epitaph

Writing

Think, *in English*, about the most similar story in your culture. Then, using the vocabulary words, write it, *in English*, in correct American form and as briefly as possible.

Speaking

Now, tell your story.

Jack and the Beanstalk

Reading Readiness

A. With a partner look at this advertisement. Describe what you see. Try to guess the names of the characters in the story and what the story will be about.

B. Look at these questions and share your ideas with the class.

1. Do children who are given everything bring their parents joy or sorrow?

2. Have you ever done a really stupid thing and had it turn out well in the end?

Jack's Organic Fertilizer

Guaranteed to Grow Vegetables as High as the Sky (And Not Just Beans!) Turn Your Garden into Gold

Available at All Fine Nurseries.

Background Notes

This is a story about a very spoiled and lazy young man who is also very curious. When opportunity comes, he takes advantage of it. The story was first written in England in 1734 and later was made popular in 1892 by Joseph Jacobs in his book *English Fairy Tales.*

Reading Selection

Now read this story once, as quickly as possible, for the general idea. Try to guess the meanings of the words you don't understand by the context. You can underline the words you don't know, but don't stop reading.

Once there was a poor widow who had only one son, named Jack, and a cow named Milky White. Now the son was not a bad boy, but he was a dreamer, and his mother spoiled him very much. One day Milky White stopped giving milk. The poor widow wrung her hands and cried, "Oh, what shall we do for food, what shall we do?" "Oh, cheer up, Mother dear," said Jack. "I'll sell Milky White at the market, and then we'll see what we can do."

So off Jack went to the market. He hadn't gone far when he met a funny looking man who said, "Hello, Jack, and where are you going?" "Well, hello," said Jack, surprised that the man knew his name. "Off to the market to sell my cow." "Well, I have some magic beans in my pocket. If you plant them overnight, they'll grow up to the sky. I'll trade you five beans for that old cow." So Jack made the trade and hurried home to his mother to show her his bargain. "What!? You've sold our cow for five beans? What a fool, what an idiot!" She threw the beans out the window and sent Jack to bed without any supper.

Jack went upstairs to his little room under the roof. He was sorry that his mother was so angry, and he was also sorry that he was hungry. Soon he fell asleep. The next morning when he awoke, his room looked strange. The bright sun was not shining in the window. It was dark. He jumped out of bed and ran to the window, and what do you think he saw? Why, the beans that his mother had thrown out the window had grown up overnight just as the man had said. The beanstalk looked just like a ladder to Jack, so he opened the window and began climbing up. He climbed and he climbed and he climbed, and he climbed and he climbed and he climbed until he reached the sky. Then he saw a long road, and he walked and walked until he came to a great, big, tall house. In front of the house was a great, big, tall woman. Well, you know how hungry the boy was. He hadn't had his dinner and he had had a long climb, so he said, "Good morning. Could you please give me some breakfast?" "Oh, so you want some breakfast?" she said. "It's breakfast you'll *be* if you don't run fast. My man is an ogre, and there's nothing he likes better than boys fried on toast." And suddenly, thump, thump,

thump, the ground began to tremble. "Oh goodness, gracious, it's my man. Quick, come into the kitchen and jump in the oven." And just as she closed the oven door the ogre came in. He was a giant and had three cows in his hand. "Here, wife, fry me a couple of these for breakfast. What do I smell? Then the ogre said,

> Fee-fi-fo-fum,
> I smell the blood of an Englishman.
> Be he alive or be he dead,
> I'll have his bones to grind my bread.

"Oh, don't be silly, my dear. You can probably still smell the little boy you ate yesterday," said the wife, and she cooked his breakfast. The ogre ate everything and then went to his gold chest and took out some bags of gold. He sat at the table and started to count his money, but after a while, his head began to nod. Soon he began to snore, and the whole house trembled. Jack crept out of the oven, ran on tiptoe, grabbed a big bag of gold, and ran as fast as he could to the beanstalk. He threw the bag to the ground and climbed down. He showed his mother the gold and said, "Well, wasn't I right about the beans?"

For a long time Jack and his mother had a lot of money, but all good things come to an end, and so did the money. Jack decided to try his luck again. So one morning he climbed and he climbed and he climbed and he climbed and he climbed and he climbed until he reached the sky. He went down the long road and he walked and walked until he came to that great, big, tall house. There was the great, big, tall woman. "Good morning. Could you please give me some breakfast?" "Aren't you the boy who came here before, the day my man lost a bag of gold? Do you know anything about it?" "I'm too hungry to talk right now," said Jack. And the ogre's wife was so curious to find out about the gold that she took him into the kitchen and gave him his breakfast. Suddenly, Jack heard thump, thump, thump, and the ground began to tremble. Jack jumped into the oven. "Here, wife, fry me a couple of these sheep for breakfast. But what do I smell?" said the giant.

> Fee-fi-fo-fum,
> I smell the blood of an Englishman.
> Be he alive or be he dead,
> I'll have his bones to grind my bread.

"Oh, nonsense, my dear. You can probably still smell the little boy you ate yesterday," said the wife, and she cooked his breakfast. The ogre ate everything and then said, "Wife, bring me the hen that lays the golden eggs." "Lay!" commanded the ogre, and before you could say one, two, three, the hen laid an egg of solid gold. Then the ogre's head began to nod. Soon he began to snore, and the whole house trembled again. Jack jumped out of the oven, grabbed the hen, and ran as fast as he could to the beanstalk. But the hen gave a cackle and woke the giant. "Wife, where is my hen?" roared the giant. And that was all Jack heard. When he reached the ground he showed his mother the hen and said, "Lay," and the hen laid an egg of gold.

But Jack was not content. "Maybe the giant has more wonderful things. I'll try my luck again." So one morning he climbed and he climbed, and he climbed and he climbed and he climbed and he climbed until he reached the sky. He went down the long road, and he walked and walked, but this time he knew better than to go straight to the ogre's house. He hid behind a bush until he saw the ogre's wife come out of the house with a pitcher to take to the well. As quick as a minute, he ran into the house and hid in a big pot in the kitchen. Soon he heard thump, thump, thump, and the ground began to tremble.

"Fee-fi-fo-fum. I smell him, wife, I smell him." "If you think it's that little rascal who stole your gold and your hen, he must be in the oven," said the wife. They looked but found nothing there. They looked everywhere, but, luckily for Jack, not in the big pot! "There you go again with your nonsense, my dear. You can probably still smell the little boy you ate yesterday," said the wife, and she cooked his breakfast. The ogre ate everything and then said, "Wife, bring me my golden harp." "Sing!" commanded the ogre, and before you could say one, two, three, the golden harp sang most beautifully. Then the ogre's head began to nod. Soon he began to snore, and the whole house trembled again. Jack crept out of the pot, as quiet as a mouse, grabbed the harp and dashed to the beanstalk. But the harp called out, "Master, Master!" and the ogre woke up just in time to see Jack running away with the harp. Well, the giant was not too happy about climbing down the beanstalk, but the harp was calling, so down he went after Jack. Jack saw his mother's garden down below and called, "Mother, Mother, bring an ax." His mother came rushing out with an ax. Jack jumped to the ground and chopped the beanstalk in two. The ogre fell down and broke his crown, and the beanstalk came tumbling after.

Then Jack showed his mother the golden harp. Now that they had the golden harp and the golden eggs, they were never poor again. Jack become so rich that he married a great princess, and they lived happily ever after.

_____

Checking Your Comprehension

Answer these questions in class.
1. Why does Jack trade Milky White for the beans?
2. How does Jack steal the bag of gold?
3. What makes the giant wake up when Jack steals the harp?
4. What happens to the giant in the end?

Be a Vocabulary Detective

Working in pairs, look for hints and guess the vocabulary from the context clues. Then fill in the blanks with the correct answers.

Clue 1

Jack didn't want the giant to wake up, so he *crept* to the table *on tiptoe*. When the giant awakened, Jack *dashed* to the beanstalk.

1. *Creep* means _____ (v).
   a) to stamp   b) to walk quietly   c) to run

2. *On tiptoe* means _____ (adv).
   a) walking flat   b) crawling   c) walking on the toes

3. *Dash* means_____ (v).
   a) to run   b) to hyphenate   c) to walk quietly

Clue 2

Jack climbs the beanstalk and goes to the house of an *ogre* who is so enormous that he makes the ground *tremble* when he walks. The ogre's head *nods* after breakfast.

4. An *ogre* is _____ (n).
   a) a liar   b) a monster   c) a fairy

5. *Tremble* means_____ (v).
   a) to shake   b) to rumble   c) to break

6. *Nod* means_____ (v).
   a) to bend one's hand   b) to bow   c) to bend one's head

Clue 3

The ogre's wife carries a *pitcher* to fill at the *well*. She thinks Jack is a *rascal* because she knows he stole the gold.

7. A *pitcher* is _____ (n).
   a) a baseball player   b) a container for water
   c) something to hang on the wall

8. A *well* is _____ (n).
   a) a place to get water from the ground   b) a water vending machine
   c) good

9. A *rascal* is _____ (n).
   a) a good person   b) an enemy   c) a trickster

Clue 4

When the hen lays the golden egg she *cackles*.

10. *Cackle* sounds like _____ (v).
    a) an airplane   b) an old door opening slowly   c) a doorbell

Clue 5

The giant's wife probably *wrung* her hands when she heard that her husband broke his *crown*.

11. *Wring* (present tense of *wrung*) means _____ (v).
    a) to twist   b) to wash   c) to cry

12. A *crown* is _____ (n).
    a) a head   b) a back   c) a foot

Questions for Discussion

First, reread the story carefully looking for the deeper meanings and reviewing the vocabulary. Then in groups of four discuss the following questions with your classmates. Be sure to tell what your native culture is.

1.   What was your favorite sentence in this story and why?
2.   Why did Jack go back the third time? Was it a wise decision?
3.   Did Jack and his mother deserve to live happily ever after?

Putting All the Pieces Together

Look at the puzzles on page 18 and page 23. Find the pieces that fit this story and discuss what cultural values this folktale teaches American children.

Double-checking the Vocabulary

Fill in the crossword with the following vocabulary words: wring, ogre, tremble, nod, creep, tiptoe, cackle, pitcher, well, rascal, dash, crown.

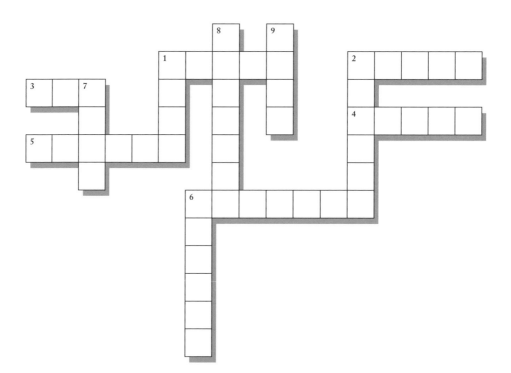

Across

1. to twist
2. to move slowly and quietly with the body close to the ground
3. to bend one's head forward and down
4. an old word for head
5. a dishonest person or a person who plays tricks
6. shake

Down

1. a place where water comes from underground
2. an unpleasant laugh, like a hen
6. to walk on one's toes with the rest of the foot not touching the ground
7. to run fast
8. a large container for storing and pouring liquid
9. a fierce creature, a monster

Writing

Think, *in English*, about the most similar story in your culture. Then, using the vocabulary words, write it, *in English*, in correct American form and as briefly as possible.

Speaking

Now, tell your story.

Chapter 8

Honesty's the Best Policy

> I hold the maxim no less applicable to public than to
> private affairs that honesty is always the best policy.
> —George Washington, Farewell Address, 1796

> When in doubt, tell the truth.
> —Mark Twain, *Pudd'nhead Wilson*, 1893

Goldilocks and the Three Bears

Reading Readiness

A. With a partner look at this advertisement. Describe what you see. Try to
    guess the names of the characters in the story and what the story will be
    about.

Goldilocks Desk Chair

Tired of Aching Backs and Necks?
Is Your Desk Chair Too Hard, Too
Soft, Too High, Too Low?
Try the Goldilocks Desk Chair,
Designed to Be JUST RIGHT™
You Can Easily Adjust the Height
of the Chair and the Firmness of
the Cushion. Guaranteed to Satisfy
Even the Most Particular.
Call 1-800-JUSTRITE
Sold at All Fine Department Stores

B. Look at these questions and share your ideas with the class.
   1. Consider these three possibilities:
      a) If a child heard a story about a little bear and a mean fox, with which character would the child identify?
      b) If a child heard a story about a little bear and an old woman, with which character would the child identify?
      c) If a child heard a story about a little bear and a little girl, with which character would the child identify?

      Now, answer this question: Would it change the lesson of a story to change the "hero"? Explain.
   2. Describe the rights of privacy in your culture.

Background Notes

This is a story from Scotland written by Elinor Mure in 1831. The story was a birthday gift for a young boy to teach him to respect others' property and privacy. The tale was originally about a fox who intrudes on three bears and is eaten up by them. In an 1856 story the fox was changed to an old woman with silver hair. In the 1904 version, the old woman was changed to a little girl with blond hair.

Reading Selection

Now read this story once, as quickly as possible, for the general idea. Try to guess the meanings of the words you don't understand by the context. You can underline the words you don't know, but don't stop reading.

Once upon a time there were three bears who lived in a cottage in the forest. There was a great, huge Father Bear with a great, huge voice, a middle-sized Mother Bear with a middle-sized voice and a wee, tiny Baby Bear with a wee, tiny voice.

One morning the middle-sized Mother Bear put the porridge on the table. "This porridge is too hot to eat," she said. "Let us go walk in the woods until it is cool."

No sooner had the three bears left their cottage than a little girl named Goldilocks came to the cottage. "I wonder who lives here?" she thought. She peeked in the window and saw no one. She peeked in the keyhole and saw no one. Then she knocked at the door. But no one answered. The door was not locked, so she went in. She saw a table with three bowls of porridge. She went to the great, huge bowl of porridge and tasted it. "This porridge is too hot." Then she went to the middle-sized bowl of porridge. "This porridge is too cold." She went to the wee, tiny bowl of porridge. "This porridge is just right." And she ate it all up.

Then Goldilocks saw three chairs. She sat in the great, huge chair. "This chair is too hard." Then she went to the middle-sized chair. "This chair is too soft." She went to the wee, tiny chair. "This chair is just right." And she sat on it, but the bottom of the chair came out and down came hers, right on the ground!

Then Goldilocks went into the bedroom and saw three beds. She lay down on the great, huge bed. "This bed is too high." Then she went to the middle-sized bed. "This bed is too low." She went to the wee, tiny bed. "This bed is just right." And she went fast asleep.

Just then the three bears returned from their walk. "Someone's been eating my porridge," said the great, huge Father Bear with a great, huge voice. "Someone's been eating my porridge." said the middle-sized Mother Bear with a middle-sized voice. "Someone's been eating my porridge and it's all gone," cried the wee, tiny Baby Bear with a wee, tiny voice.

"Someone's been sitting in my chair," said the great, huge Father Bear with a great, huge voice. "Someone's been sitting in my chair," said the middle-sized Mother Bear with a middle-sized voice. "Someone's been sitting in my chair and it's all broken," cried the wee, tiny Baby Bear with a wee, tiny voice.

"Someone's been sleeping in my bed," said the great, huge Father Bear with a great, huge voice. "Someone's been sleeping in my bed," said the middle-sized Mother Bear with a middle-sized voice. "Someone's been sleeping in my bed and there she is!" cried the wee, tiny Baby Bear with a wee, tiny voice.

At this, Goldilocks woke up and jumped out of the bed and out of the window as fast as she could. And the three bears never saw anything more of her.

Checking Your Comprehension

Answer these questions in class.
1. Why were the bears upset?
2. Why did Goldilocks leave so quickly?
3. What kind of voice does the little bear have? Why?

Be a Vocabulary Detective

Working in pairs, look for hints and guess the vocabulary from the context clues. Then fill in the blanks with the correct answers.

Clue 1

The family of bears lives in a small *cottage*. At breakfast, the *porridge* is too hot to eat so they go for a walk in the forest.

1. A *cottage* is _____ (n).
   a) a castle   b) a zoo   c) a small house

2. *Porridge* is _____ (n).
   a) ice cream   b) hot cereal   c) a doughnut

Clue 2

The Baby Bear is *wee, tiny*. The Father Bear is *huge*.

3. *Wee, tiny* means _____ (adj).
   a) very fat   b) very small   c) very large

4. *Huge* means _____ (adj).
   a) very large   b) very small   c) putting arms around someone

Clue 3

Goldilocks wonders who lives in the cottage so she *peeks* through the *keyhole* of the door.

5. *Peek* means _____ (v).
   a) to knock   b) to look   c) to lock

6. A *keyhole* is _____ (n).
   a) a window   b) a chimney   c) a lock

Questions for Discussion

First, reread the story carefully looking for the deeper meanings and reviewing the vocabulary. Then in groups of four discuss the following questions with your classmates. Be sure to tell what your native culture is.

1. What was your favorite sentence in this story and why?
2. What kind of person is Goldilocks?
3. Did you understand the language "joke," "And she sat on it, but the bottom of the chair came out and down came hers, right on the ground!" Explain the joke.
4. Look at this cartoon. Do you think it is funny? Explain why or why not.

For Better or for Worse, Lynn Johnston Prod., Inc. Reprinted with permission of Universal Press Syndicate. All rights reserved.

Putting All the Pieces Together

Look at the puzzles on page 18 and page 23. Find the pieces that fit this story and discuss what cultural values this folktale teaches American children.

Double-checking the Vocabulary

Look at the definitions and cross out the words in the list that match. Then, looking at the words that remain, read from left to right, top to bottom, and find the answer to the question, "Why did Goldilocks leave so fast?"

a. very large, enormous
b. a small house
c. very small
d. to look when you shouldn't
e. a hot cereal made of boiled grains
f. the opening in the lock for the key

wee, tiny	it	porridge
was	cottage	peek
so	beary	keyhole
scary	huge	there

Writing

Think, *in English*, about the most similar story in your culture. Then, using the vocabulary words, write it, *in English*, in correct American form and as briefly as possible.

Speaking

Now, tell your story.

The Pied Piper of Hamelin

Reading Readiness

A. With a partner look at this advertisement. Describe what you see. Try to guess the names of the characters in the story and what the story will be about.

B. Look at these questions and share your ideas with the class.
   1. What happens if you hire someone to do a job, he does it, and then you decide not to pay him for the work?
   2. Have you ever known anyone who has had a serious problem with rats in his or her house? How did he or she get rid of them?

Background Notes

This is from an old German legend made quite popular in the English language in 1842 when a very famous poet, Robert Browning, wrote a poem about the legend as a gift for a sick child. It became Browning's most popular poem and was soon turned into story form and told to generations of English speaking children. The story that you will now read is retold from the original poem. (*Note:* since this is from the old German story, the name for their dollars is "guilders.")

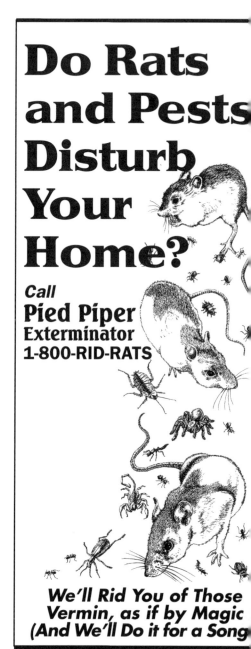

Do Rats and Pests Disturb Your Home?

Call **Pied Piper Exterminator 1-800-RID-RATS**

We'll Rid You of Those Vermin, as if by Magic (And We'll Do it for a Song

Reading Selection

Now read this story once, as quickly as possible, for the general idea. Try to guess the meanings of the words you don't understand by the context. You can underline the words you don't know, but don't stop reading.

In 1294, in the town of Hamelin in Germany, a most horrible catastrophe occurred. Hamelin was a very pleasant town on the banks of the River Wester, and the townsfolk were lucky to live there. But suddenly there was a terrible infestation of pests. Rats! Rats everywhere. They bit the dogs and killed the cats and bit the babies in their beds. They ate all the cheeses and even licked the soup from the cooks' spoons. They made their nests in the hats of the men, and the women couldn't even chat with each other for the shrieking and squeaking of the rats.

At last the people gathered at the town hall and threatened to fire the mayor and city council if they did not solve the problem. The mayor and council went into their office and sat and thought and tried to find an answer when suddenly there was a tapping on their door. The strangest looking man came in. He was wearing a long weird coat from his head to his toes; half of it was yellow, the other half was red. He was tall and thin with sharp blue eyes, light loose hair, and tan skin. He had no hair on his face. He smiled broadly as he said, "Please, Your Honors, I possess a secret charm that allows me to cause all living creatures to follow after me. I usually use my charms on creatures that do people harm. They call me the Pied Piper." And the lord mayor noticed that a pipe hung from a yellow and red scarf around the Piper's neck. "So if you will give me one thousand guilders, I shall draw the rats out of Hamelin town." "What! one thousand! We will give you fifty thousand!" said the happy mayor and council.

So the Piper stepped into the street, smiled, and picked up his pipe. After the first three notes the people heard the strangest noises, like a muttering that grew to a grumbling and then a mighty rumbling, and out of the houses came the rats—great rats, small rats, lean rats, fat rats, brown rats, black rats, gray rats, yellow rats, old rats, young rats, father rats, mother rats, uncle rats, cousin rats, families of rats by tens, brothers, sisters, husbands, wives all followed the Piper. He traveled through the whole of Hamelin with the rats following and led them to the River Wester where they all plunged in and perished.

Well, you should have seen the townsfolk. They rang the bells and gathered in the marketplace to dance and celebrate. Suddenly the Pied Piper arrived. "First, if you please, my thousand guilders!"

The mayor and the council looked solemn. They did not want to pay this large sum to a wandering fellow with such strange clothes! The mayor said, "We saw the rats sink in the river, and what's dead can't come back to life. We were just joking when we said we would give you a thousand guilders. We'll give you fifty."

The Piper looked very disappointed. "A deal's a deal. You must pay what you owe. Folks who put me in a passion may find me pipe after another fashion."

"I'm not afraid of you," cried the mayor. "How dare you threaten us? Do your worst, go blow your pipe until you burst!"

So once more the Piper stepped into the street, smiled, and picked up his pipe. Three sweet, soft notes came out, and suddenly you could hear the sounds of small feet pattering and little hands clapping and little tongues chattering, and all the little children of Hamelin came running—all the little boys and girls with rosy cheeks and yellow curls and sparkling eyes and teeth like pearls. And the Piper traveled through the whole of Hamelin with the children following, and then, at the River Wester, he turned to Koppleberg Hill. All the parents and the mayor were relieved. "He can never cross that mighty top. So we shall see our children stop." But when the children reached the mountainside, a huge door magically opened! The Piper went in with all the children following, and then the door shut fast. Did I say all? No! One child was lame, and he could not go as fast as the others. And in later years he would say, "It's so dull in our town since my playmates left. And I can't forget all the wonderful things the Piper promised us, for he said he would lead us to a joyous land of tame animals and good food and toys, and that my lame foot would be cured."

And the people of Hamelin looked high and low for their children and the Piper. They offered huge rewards, but they never saw their children again. They wrote the story down and put it on the mountainside and on the town gate and on the church door, and they warned everyone that if you give a promise you must keep it because you must always pay the Piper.

Checking Your Comprehension

Answer these questions in class.
1. Describe what the Piper looks like.
2. How does the Piper get rid of the rats?
3. Why does the mayor not pay the Piper?
4. What happens to the children?

Be a Vocabulary Detective

Working in pairs, look for hints and guess the vocabulary from the context clues. Then fill in the blanks with the correct answers.

Clue 1

The lovely town of Hamelin had a sudden *catastrophe,* for it was suddenly full of rats. There were not a few rats, or even some rats, but an *infestation* of those terrible, dirty *pests.*

1. A *catastrophe* is _____ (n).
   a) a party   b) the flu   c) a terrible event

2. An *infestation* is _____ (n).
   a) a disease   b) large numbers   c) a war

3. A *pest* is _____ (n).
   a) a good friend   b) an annoyance   c) a pet

Clue 2

There are a lot of words to describe sound in this story. The women meet together to *chat.* But they can't hear themselves because the rats are making a lot of noise. Think about all the possible sounds that rats can make. It might help to say the words out loud and listen to the different sounds the words make. One or two rats will *squeak.* Many rats will argue with each other, and there will be a loud *shrieking.* When the Piper first calls the rats to follow, there is a low sound of *muttering.* When some of the rats sound angry as they run out into the street there is the sound of *grumbling.* When all the rats run into the street it is as if a big train is coming through town, for the townsfolk hear a great *rumbling.*

4. *Chat* means _____ (v).
   a) to argue   b) to sing   c) to talk

5. To *squeak* is to make a sound like _____ (v).
   a) new shoes   b) a drum   c) a lion

6. To *shriek* is to make a sound like _____ (v).
   a) thunder   b) a car   c) a frightened monkey

7. To *mutter* is to make a sound like _____ (v).
   a) a person talking   b) a bird   c) a piano
   quietly in church

8. To *grumble* is to make a sound like _____ (v).
   a) a spider   b) a complaining person   c) an airplane

9. To *rumble* is to make a sound like _____ (v).
   a) a hungry stomach   b) a dog   c) a violin

Clue 3

The Pied Piper is dressed in a very *weird* way. He is wearing an irregularly colored (pied) coat. His appearance is very extraordinary.

10. *Weird* means_____ (adj).
    a) fashionable   b) strange   c) expensive

Clue 4

The rats *plunged* into the River Wester and drowned. Not one rat was left. They had all *perished*.

11. *Plunge* means _____ (v).
    a) to fly   b) to jump deep in   c) to drink

12. *Perish* means _____ (v).
    a) to swim   b) to live   c) to die

Clue 5

The Pied Piper is very angry because the mayor will not honor his promise. The Piper warns the mayor that people who put him in a *passion* will be sorry.

13. *Passion* means_____ (n).
    a) a deep uncontrollable feeling   b) hunger   c) happiness

Clue 6

One child is left to come back and tell the people of Hamelin what happened to their children. He couldn't follow fast enough to get into the mountain because of his *lame* leg.

14. *Lame* means _____ (adj).
    a) thin   b) hurt   c) large

Questions for Discussion

First, reread the story carefully looking for the deeper meanings and reviewing the vocabulary. Then in groups of four discuss the following questions with your classmates. Be sure to tell what your native culture is.

1. What was your favorite sentence in this story and why?
2. Do you think the Piper did the right thing? (Did the punishment fit the crime?)
3. Do you understand the expression "you must pay the Piper"?

Putting All the Pieces Together

Look at the puzzles on page 18 and page 23. Find the pieces that fit this story and discuss what cultural values this folktale teaches American children.

Double-checking the Vocabulary

Match the definitions with the words.

a. to push, jump, or move suddenly deep into something
b. to talk in a friendly, informal manner
c. to die, to be completely destroyed
d. not able to walk well due to a weakness of the leg or foot
e. a sudden, unexpected event that causes great pain and suffering
f. to cry out with a high sound
g. a small insect or animal that annoys and destroys
h. extremely strange, unnatural
i. to make a deep, loud continuing sound, like thunder
j. presence in large, troublesome numbers
k. a strong, deep, often uncontrollable feeling of love, hatred, or anger
l. to make a low sound expressing discontent and dissatisfaction
m. to complain in a low voice, not easily heard or understood
n. to make a short, very high, but not loud sound

1. a catastrophe
2. an infestation
3. pest
4. to chat
5. to shriek
6. to squeak
7. weird
8. to mutter
9. to grumble
10. to rumble
11. to plunge
12. to perish
13. a passion
14. lame

Writing

Think, *in English*, about the most similar story in your culture. Then, using the vocabulary words, write it, *in English*, in correct American form and as briefly as possible.

Speaking

Now, tell your story.

Rumpelstiltskin

Reading Readiness

A. With a partner look at this advertisement. Describe what you see. Try to
   guess the names of the characters in the
   story and what the story will be about.
B. Look at these questions and share your
   ideas with the class.
   1. What happens when you are too
      proud and too sure of yourself?
   2. What is the strangest name you
      have ever heard? Do you know the
      meaning of it?

> **RUMPELSTILTSKIN
> EMPLOYMENT AGENCY**
>
> No Job Too Hard to Find the
> Perfect Employee for You
> Even If You Need to Hire Someone
> to Spin Straw into Gold!
> Give Us the Task, We'll Find the
> Person to Do It.
> Call 1-800-WE-FIND-4-U

Background Notes

This is a story about a young woman who has a very selfish father who lies. A
money-loving king forces her to take straw and turn it into gold. If she doesn't
do it, she will die. This is an ancient story that originally stressed both the
danger of boasting and the power of one's name. The story was collected, in this
newer form, by the Brothers Grimm in Germany in the early 1800s.

Reading Selection

Now read this story once, as quickly as possible, for the general idea. Try to guess the meanings of the words you don't understand by the context. You can underline the words you don't know, but don't stop reading.

There was once a miller who was very poor; his only wealth was his one beautiful daughter. One day he came to speak with the king, and, to make himself important, he told the king that he had a daughter who could spin gold out of straw.

The king said to the miller, "This is a talent that pleases me well. If your daughter is as clever as you say, bring her to my castle tomorrow, so I may put her to the test."

When the girl was brought to the king, he led her to a room that was quite full of straw. He gave her a wheel and a spindle and said, "Now set to work, and if by the early morning you have not spun this straw to gold, you shall die." And he shut the door himself and left her there alone.

And so the poor miller's daughter was left sitting there. She could not think what to do, and she had no idea of how to spin gold from straw. Her distress grew so great that she began to weep.

Then all at once the door opened, and in came a funny looking little man who said, "Good evening, miller's daughter. Why are you crying?"

"Oh!" answered the girl, "I have to spin gold out of straw, and I don't understand how to do it."

Then the little man said, "What will you give me if I spin it for you?"

"My necklace," said the girl.

The little man took the necklace, sat behind the wheel, took up a handful of straw, and whirr, whirr, whirr! three times the wheel went round and the straw had turned into gold thread. Then he took up another pile of straw, and whirr, whirr, whirr! three times the wheel went round and the straw had turned into gold thread. And so he went on till morning, when all the straw had been spun and all the room was full of spools of gold thread.

The king came at dawn. When he saw the gold he was astonished, and he rejoiced, for he was very greedy. He had the miller's daughter taken into another room filled with straw, much bigger than the last, and told her that if she valued her life, she must spin it all in one night.

The girl did not know what to do, so she began to cry. The door opened, and the little man appeared again. "What will you give me if I spin all this straw into gold?"

"The ring from my finger," said the girl.

So the little man took the ring and began to set the wheel whirring around. By the next morning all the straw had been spun into glistening gold.

The king rejoiced at the sight, but he could never have enough gold. He had the miller's daughter taken into a still larger room filled with straw and said, "This, too, must be spun in one night, and if you accomplish this, you shall be my wife." For he thought, "Although she is but a miller's daughter, I am not likely to find anyone richer in the whole world."

As soon as the girl was left alone, the little man appeared for the third time and said, "What will you give me if I spin the straw for you this time?"

"I have nothing left to give," said the girl.

"Then you must promise me the first child you have after you are queen," said the little man.

"But who knows whether that will happen?" thought the girl. She did not know what else to do, so she promised the little man what he desired. Then he began to spin until the straw was gold. In the morning the king came in and found all done according to his wishes. He immediately married the miller's pretty daughter, and she became his queen.

In a year's time a fine child was born to the queen. She thought no more of the little man; but one day he came suddenly into her room and said, "Now give me what you promised."

The queen was greatly terrified and offered the little man all the riches of the kingdom if he would not take her child. But the little man said, "No, I would rather have something living than all the treasures of the world."

The queen began to lament and to weep so that the little man had pity on her.

"I will give you three days," he said, "and if at the end of that time you cannot tell me my name, you must give the child to me."

The queen spent the whole night thinking over all the names that she had ever heard. She also sent a messenger through the land to ask far and wide for all the names that could be found. And when the little man came the next day she repeated all the names she knew, beginning with

Tom, John, and Michael, and she went through the whole list to Caspar, Theophilus, and Balthazar. But after each name the little man said, "That is not my name."

The second day the queen asked all the neighbors what their servants' names were, and she told the little man all the most unusual names, saying, "Perhaps you are called Roast-Ribs, or Crooked-Legs, or Fiddle-Sticks?"

He answered nothing but "That is not my name." The third day the messenger came back again and said, "I have not been able to find one single new name. But as I passed through the woods I came to a high hill, and near it was a little house. Before the house burned a fire, and around the fire danced a comical little man who hopped on one leg and cried,

> Oh what a lovely feast I'll make,
> Today I'll brew, tomorrow I'll bake.
> Today I'll dance and laugh and sing,
> Tomorrow the Queen's child they'll bring.
> Little does my lady dream
> That Rumpelstiltskin is my name!

When the queen heard this she jumped for joy. Soon afterward, the little man walked in and said, "Now, Mrs. Queen, what is my name? She said at first, "Are you called Jack?"

"No," he answered.

"Are you called Harry?" she asked again.

"No," he answered. And then she said, "Then perhaps your name is Rumpelstiltskin!"

"The devil told you that! The devil told you that!" cried the little man, and in his anger he stamped with his right foot so hard that it went into the ground above his knee. Then he seized his left foot with both hands in such a fury that he split in two, and that was the end of him.

Checking Your Comprehension

Answer these questions in class.

1. Why does the miller lie to the king about his daughter's talents?
2. Why does the girl promise her child to the little man?
3. Why did Rumpelstiltskin want the queen's child?

Be a Vocabulary Detective

Working in pairs, look for hints and guess the vocabulary from the context clues. Then fill in the blanks with the correct answers.

Clue 1

The miller's daughter is put in a horrible situation. She will die unless she turns the straw into gold, and she has no magical powers. Of course, she feels great *distress* to be in such a terrible situation. Her eyes fill with tears and she *weeps*. When Rumpelstiltskin comes to take her baby, she is so full of sorrow and sadness that she *laments*.

1. *Distress* is _____ (n).
   a) happiness   b) surprise   c) anxiety

2. *Weep* means _____ (v).
   a) to cry   b) to laugh   c) to sneeze

3. *Lament* means _____ (v).
   a) to wail   b) to giggle   c) to blush

Clue 2

The king values money more than the miller's daughter's life. He is very *greedy*. When he sees that the miller's daughter can really spin straw into gold he is *astonished*. He is so delighted with the money that he *rejoices*.

4. *Greedy* is_____ (adj).
   a) wanting more   b) wanting less   c) generous

5. *Astonished* means _____ (adj).
   a) surprised   b) sad   c) frightened

6. *Rejoice* means _____ (v).
   a) to cry   b) to argue   c) to cheer

Clue 3

Rumpelstiltskin is very *comical* looking. He knows how to use a spinning wheel to turn straw into beautiful, shining gold thread. He sits at the spinning wheel and makes it go around and around very fast. The miller's daughter hears *whirr, whirr, whirr* and sees the gold thread wrap around the *spool* and *glisten* in the light of dawn.

7. *Comical* means_____ (adj).
   a) funny   b) handsome   c) small

8. *Whirr* is the sound of _____ (n).
    a) water   b) bells   c) movement

9. A *spool* is a _____ (n).
    a) something round   b) something square   c) something triangular

10. *Glisten* means _____ (v).
    a) to shine   b) to drip   c) to disappear

11. *Dawn* is _____ (n).
    a) noon   b) sunset   c) sunrise

Clue 4

Rumpelstiltskin was very sure that no one would know his name. He was so angry that the queen found out that he was full of *fury*. He *stamped* his foot so hard on the ground that it went in. He *seized* the other leg and pulled so hard, he split in two.

12. *Fury* is _____ (n).
    a) great sadness   b) great anger   c) great surprise

13. *Stamp* means _____ (v).
    a) to hit with the bottom of a foot   b) to place gently   c) to hop

14. *Seize* means _____ (v).
    a) to push   b) to grab   c) to throw

Questions for Discussion

First, reread the story carefully looking for the deeper meanings and reviewing the vocabulary. Then in groups of four discuss the following questions with your classmates. Be sure to tell what your native culture is.
1. What was your favorite sentence in this story and why?
2. Do you think Rumpelstiltskin was justly punished?
3. Was the queen fair to Rumpelstiltskin?

Putting All the Pieces Together

Look at the puzzles on page 18 and page 23. Find the pieces that fit this story and discuss what cultural values this folktale teaches American children.

Double-checking the Vocabulary

Look at the definitions and cross out the words in the list that match. Then, looking at the words that remain, read from left to right, top to bottom, and find the answer to the question, "What do Rumpelstiltskin and the postal clerk have in common?"

a. strong anger
b. to be greatly surprised
c. funny
d. great suffering
e. wanting to have more than you need
f. to cry
g. a sound of fast movement
h. to grab with great power
i. to feel great happiness
j. sunrise
k. to express grief or sorrow
l. an object upon which thread is wrapped
m. shining

to be astonished	they	distress	spool
whirr	stamp	greedy	too much
weep	dawn	glistening	lament
comical	seize	fury	rejoice

Writing

Think, *in English*, about the most similar story in your culture. Then, using the vocabulary words, write it, *in English*, in correct American form and as briefly as possible.

Speaking

Now, tell your story.

The Emperor's New Clothes

Reading Readiness

A. With a partner look at this advertisement. Describe what you see. Try to guess the names of the characters in the story and what the story will be about.

B. Look at these questions and share your ideas with the class.
1. Have you ever believed something was wrong when everyone else thought it was right? Did you tell people your opinion, or were you afraid they would think you were stupid?
2. What kind of person speaks his or her mind without fear of others' laughter?

The Emperor Has No Clothes

By William J. Heffernan

Now on the Best-seller List

A Riveting Documentary of the Watergate Scandal and the Nixon Cover-up. Don't Miss the Latest Information on How Many People Knew the Truth But Were Afraid to Tell, Leading to the Downfall of an American President and a Shadow on the American Dream.

Background Notes

This is a very famous story written by Hans Christian Andersen of Denmark in 1836. It was translated into English in 1846. The theme of the story, deception, was a common folklore theme, but Andersen added his own surprise ending. To make this story easier to understand, you should remember that a long time ago clothing was made by hand and that the fabric, the material, also was made by hand. If you grew cotton or took wool from a sheep or silk from a silkworm, how would you make it into thread to make it into cloth? What tools would you use?

Reading Selection

Now read this story once, as quickly as possible, for the general idea. Try to guess the meanings of the words you don't understand by the context. You can underline the words you don't know, but don't stop reading.

Once upon a time there lived an emperor who *loved* new clothes. He had clothes for every hour of the day and evening. Whenever anyone wanted to know where he was, he or she would look in his dressing room.

One day two wicked men came to town. They said they were weavers and that they were so talented that they could make a very special cloth, so special that it was invisible to people who were stupid. That pleased the emperor very much. "Ah, if I wear that suit, I'll be able to tell the wise men from the fools," he thought.

The weavers wanted to start work immediately. They put up two looms. "We need gold and silk to spin the threads to make this special suit," the weavers said. And the emperor gave them lots and lots of gold thread to make their special cloth.

But the wicked weavers stole the gold thread and hid it in their bags. Then they pretended to make the special cloth. The weavers worked very hard moving the looms that make cloth. They bent over the looms and made them go back and forth.

One night the emperor wanted to know how the gold cloth looked. He sent his prime minister to have a look. "Go and see if the cloth is beautiful," ordered the emperor.

The prime minister went to see the weavers. They were working very hard. The prime minister looked and looked at the looms. "Oh, dear!" he thought. "I can't see anything. But *I* am not stupid." So he said to the weavers, "It's beautiful cloth. The pattern is quite charming. I'll go and tell the emperor, and he will be very pleased."

When he had gone, the weavers laughed and laughed.

The prime minister told the emperor that the cloth was very beautiful. Soon everyone was talking about the emperor's new suit. The wicked weavers told the emperor, "We need some more gold thread to finish making this special cloth." The emperor let them have lots more gold thread. But the wicked weavers stole the thread and hid it in their bags. Then they pretended to work harder than ever.

The next night, the emperor wanted someone else to look at the cloth for his new suit. This time he sent his general to have a look. "Go and see if the cloth is beautiful," ordered the emperor.

The general went to see the weavers. They looked like they were working very hard. The general looked and looked at the looms. "Oh, dear!" he thought, "I can't see anything. But *I* am not stupid." So he said to the weavers, "It's beautiful cloth. The pattern is quite charming. I'll go and tell the emperor, and he will be very pleased."

When he had gone, the weavers laughed and laughed.

The general told the emperor that the cloth was very beautiful.

Soon the weavers said that the special cloth was made. Now they pretended to cut the cloth into pieces. They began to sew the pieces together to make the emperor's new suit of clothes. The next day the weavers said, "Can the emperor come and try on his new suit?"

The emperor was very pleased. He went to see the weavers with two faithful officials. "Oh, the cloth is magnificent!" the officials said. "What!" said the emperor to himself, "I can't see the cloth! The prime minister, the general, and my officials can see it. Am *I* stupid?" So the emperor said, "This is beautiful cloth. These will be my very best clothes. As soon as the suit is ready we will have a grand parade, and I shall show the suit to all my subjects."

When the suit was ready to try on, the weavers made the emperor take off all his clothes. He had to stand quite still. They pretended to put the clothes on the emperor. "Here are the trousers, here is the shirt, here is the jacket," they said. The emperor felt very cold. He couldn't feel the clothes at all, but he said, "This is a beautiful suit of clothes. The cloth is as light as a spider's web. I can hardly feel it." The prime minister said, "It's a wonderful new suit." The general said, "I have never seen such beautiful clothes." The two faithful officials said, "The emperor has never looked more distinguished."

Everyone in the land had heard about the new suit. They all went to see the parade. The weavers made sure the emperor's suit was just right, and then they put his crown on his head. "Your Majesty, you look wonderful!" said the weavers. And the emperor gave the weavers two big bags of gold. The emperor was very, very pleased with his new clothes. "All the people will look at me," he said to himself. He went out to join the parade.

The people stood at the sides of the roads waiting for the emperor to pass by. Then the parade started, and all the people began to shout and wave. Everyone had heard about the special cloth. They had been told that only stupid people could not see it.

"The emperor's new clothes are magnificent," said a young woman.

"Absolutely charming," said an old man.

"The emperor has never looked better," said another man.

The emperor was very happy. "These are the best clothes I've ever had," he said. He laughed and waved to all the people, and they waved back to him. The parade was nearly over. The emperor thought it had been the best day of his life.

Then suddenly a little boy pointed at the emperor. The boy began to laugh. "The emperor has nothing on!" he shouted. And all the people began to laugh too.

The emperor knew that he had been tricked. "I *am* very stupid," he thought. His face turned very, very red.

And the wicked weavers? Well, of course, they were gone!

_____

Checking Your Comprehension

Answer these questions in class.
1. Why did the weavers come to town?
2. Why didn't the prime minister and the general tell the emperor the truth?
3. Why did the emperor walk naked in the parade?
4. Why did the little boy say that the emperor had no clothes?

Be a Vocabulary Detective

Working in pairs, look for hints and guess the vocabulary from the context clues. Then fill in the blanks with the correct answers.

Clue 1

Two very dishonest and *wicked* men come into town. They say they are *weavers* and they can make very special cloth. The weavers are very *clever*. They know that the emperor loves new clothes, and they know that most human beings are afraid of being thought stupid by others.

1. *Wicked* means_____ (adj).
   a) beautiful   b) nice   c) very bad

2. *Weavers* are _____ (n).
   a) teachers   b) cloth makers   c) cooks

3. *Clever* means_____ (adj).
   a) stupid   b) smart   c) boring

Clue 2

The weavers know they can get a lot of gold if they claim that they can make the clothes out of gold. They ask the emperor for the basic materials so they can make the cloth. They need gold *thread*. To make the thread, they need to *spin* the gold. Then they will make the cloth on *looms*.

4. *Thread* is _____ (n).
   a) a fine string   b) food   c) a mineral

5. *Spin* is _____ (v).
   a) to smile   b) to turn quickly   c) to stick

6. A *loom* is _____ (n).
   a) a car   b) a machine to weave cloth   c) money from the bank

Clue 3

How can the weavers make a lot of money fast? Remember, they are clever and they understand human nature. So, they just *pretend* to be working on the looms. Everyone is afraid to say that the thread is *invisible*, because then others will think that they are stupid.

7. To *pretend* is _____ (v).
   a) to love   b) to make believe   c) to blush

8. *Invisible* means _____ (adj).
   a) not seen   b) not known   c) undivided

Clue 4

The weavers claim that the emperor's clothes are the most special in the world. The *pattern* would probably be a repeat of a very special design. The clothes are so beautiful and *charming*, that they are perfect for an emperor. They are truly *magnificent*. The emperor will look very *distinguished* in those clothes.

9. A *pattern* is _____ (n).
   a) a noise   b) a color   c) a design

10. *Charming* is _____ (adj).
    a) delightful   b) terrible   c) ordinary

11. *Magnificent* is _____ (adj).
    a) terrible   b) small   c) grand

12. *Distinguished* is _____ (adj).
    a) excellent   b) dirty   c) expensive

Clue 5

The emperor hopes to find out that his ministers are *wise* and his enemies are *fools*.

13. *Wise* means_____ (adj).
    a) intelligent   b) honest   c) good

14. A *fool* is _____ (n).
    a) a funny person   b) a stupid person   c) a dishonest person

Questions for Discussion

First, reread the story carefully looking for the deeper meanings and reviewing the vocabulary. Then in groups of four discuss the following questions with your classmates. Be sure to tell what your native culture is.
1. What was your favorite sentence in this story and why?
2. Why is it only the child who tells the truth?
3. Abraham Lincoln, the sixteenth president of the United States, said, "You can fool all of the people some of the time and some of the people all of the time, but you can't fool all of the people all of the time." Do you think that quote applies to this story? Why? Why not?

Putting All the Pieces Together

Look at the puzzles on page 18 and page 23. Find the pieces that fit this story and discuss what cultural values this folktale teaches American children.

Double-checking the Vocabulary

Look at the definitions and cross out the words in the list that match. Then, looking at the words that remain, read from left to right, top to bottom, and find the answer to the question, "What did the emperor say he was wearing?"

a. to make believe something is true when it isn't
b. marked by excellent quality
c. knowledgeable through experience
d. fantastic, glorious, wonderful
e. a movable frame or machine that combines threads to turn them into cloth
f. people who make cloth with a loom
g. a regularly repeated arrangement of lines, shapes, etc.
h. not seen
i. a stupid person, an idiot
j. a very fine string made by spinning cotton, wool, silk, etc.
k. pleasing, delightful
l. evil
m. having a quick, able mind
n. to make thread by twisting

I	wicked	weavers	clever
am	wearing	invisible	my
thread	pretend	loom	charming
pattern	birthday	magnificent	distinguished
suit	wise	fool	spin

Writing

Think, *in English*, about the most similar story in your culture. Then, using the vocabulary words, write it, *in English*, in correct American form and as briefly as possible.

Speaking

Now, tell your story.

Pinocchio

Reading Readiness

A. With a partner look at this book cover. Describe what you see. Try to guess
the names of the characters in the story and what the story will be about.

B. Look at these questions and share your ideas with the class.
1. What happens to children who don't obey their parents?
2. What happens to children who have bad companions?

Background Notes

The Adventures of Pinocchio: The Story of a Puppet was written in Italy by Carlo
Lorenzini (using the pen name C. Collodi) in 1883 and is considered one of the
world's best known fantasies. It was translated into English in 1892. In 1940

Walt Disney made an animated film called *Pinocchio*. You might want to watch the video after you read the story.

Reading Selection

Now read this story once, as quickly as possible, for the general idea. Try to guess the meanings of the words you don't understand by the context. You can underline the words you don't know, but don't stop reading.

Once upon a time there was a piece of wood, a common log, and one day a carpenter decided to make it into the leg of a table. But, when the carpenter lifted his hatchet, he heard a little voice say, "Please be careful! Do not hit me so hard!" The carpenter thought it was the wind, so he hit the wood hard. "Oh, oh! You hurt me!" cried the little voice. The carpenter fainted, and at that very instant the carpenter's friend, Geppetto, came in. Geppetto was a wood-carver, and he took the log home. He made it into a marionette that he called Pinocchio. Geppetto was very surprised when he made the eyes, for they moved around and then stared at him. He made the nose, and it grew and grew and grew. He made the mouth, and it started to laugh. He made the arms and the legs, and the little puppet ran out the door and down the street. The police thought that the puppet was running away because his master, Geppetto, had beaten him, so they came and put Geppetto in prison.

Pinocchio went back home and was delighted to find the house empty. Then he heard someone saying, "cri-cri-cri." "Who's that?" "I am the Talking Cricket. I have been living in this room for more than one hundred years, and I must tell you a great truth. Woe to little boys who refuse to obey their parents and run away from home. They will never be happy in this world, and when they are older they will be sorry. If you do not go to school you will be a perfect donkey, and everyone will laugh at you. That is my advice." "Oh, I will teach you a lesson, too, Cricket," said Pinocchio, and he threw a hammer at the cricket. I do not know if he thought he would hit it, but he did and, sad to tell, the poor cricket fell from the wall, dead.

The next few days Pinocchio was very miserable. He was very hungry and lonely and cold. He lit a fire and fell asleep, but his feet were too near the coals and they started to burn. Pinocchio woke just in time and plunged his feet into water. Just then Geppetto came home from prison. He hugged Pinocchio, who said, "Oh, I am so sorry. I will go to school and learn a trade and be the comfort of your old age." Geppetto made Pinocchio new feet after he promised never to run away again. Geppetto also sold his only coat to buy Pinocchio his ABC book for school.

But on his way to school, Pinocchio saw a Marionette Theater and sold his ABC book to buy a ticket. He was captured and forced to work like a slave in the theater for many days. When he finally told his story to the owner, the owner said, "Here are five gold pieces to take to your dear father, Geppetto. Poor fellow, I feel sorry for him. Go back to him with my kindest regards."

Pinocchio was very eager to go back home and be a good son, but on his way home he met a Cat and a Fox who were swindlers. "What do you have in your hand?" they asked. "I have five pieces of gold, and I will buy a fine coat for my father and an ABC book for myself. I want to go to school and study hard. I have been a bad son, and the Talking Cricket was right. I am not happy, and I have learned this at my own expense," said Pinocchio. "But we can help you turn your five gold pieces into two thousand," the Cat and Fox said. "There is a Field of Wonders. You dig a hole and bury the gold, and the next day the gold grows into a beautiful tree loaded with gold pieces. We will show you the way." As they walked to the Field of Wonders it grew dark. Pinocchio saw the ghost of the Talking Cricket, who said, "Do not listen to bad advice. You will be sorry. Remember that boys who insist on having their own way sooner or later will come to grief." But Pinocchio would not listen to the ghost, and that night the Cat and the Fox hit Pinocchio on the head, tied a rope around his neck, and hung him from a tree. As death crept near, Pinocchio said, "Oh Father, dear Father, if you were only here," and closed his eyes.

Luckily for him, a lovely woman with blue hair (who was a fairy) saw him hanging from the tree and sent a bird to cut him down. Pinocchio was brought to her house, and he soon recovered. He did not want to tell the beautiful fairy the real story of what had happened. But when Pinocchio made up a story about his adventures, his nose kept on growing longer and longer, and the fairy started to laugh. "Lies, my boy, are known in a moment," she said, and so he told her the truth. "Money must be made honestly. One must work and know how to earn it with hand or brain," she said, and then she sent for a woodpecker to fly in and make Pinocchio's nose smaller again.

Pinocchio set off once again for home. On the way he heard some very sad news. His father, Geppetto, had been looking all over for his son. Geppeto had gone off in a little boat that had sunk in the water and had never been seen again. Pinocchio went back to the fairy to see if she could help. "You must do it yourself," she said. "You are lazy, but it is never too late to learn. A man, whether rich or poor, should do something in this world. No one can find happiness without work." "I want to become a real boy and find my father, and I promise I will work and study and be obedient," said Pinocchio. And this time his nose didn't grow.

And so Pinocchio went off to school, and he studied hard. His teachers were very proud of him. He had many friends, but some of them were well known rascals. "Take care, Pinocchio," the teacher said. "Those bad companions will sooner or later lead you into trouble." "Oh, there's no such danger," said Pinocchio. "I am too wise."

But the very next day the rascals, led by a boy named Lamp-Wick, told Pinocchio that they were skipping school to go to the beach where an enormous shark had been seen. "Oh, maybe that is the one who was seen the day my father's boat was lost. I can always go to school." So Pinocchio went off with them.

They told him that there was a special land called the Land of the Toys where children could play all day; there was no school and no rules. Pinocchio decided to go with them. They found a cart pulled by twenty-four donkeys, and Pinocchio rode on a donkey. As they were going to the Land of Toys he heard someone whisper, "Boys who stop studying to give their time to play will sooner or later come to grief. A day will come when you will weep as bitterly as I, and it will be too late." And Pinocchio saw tears coming out of the donkey's eyes, but he thought that it was because of the wind.

For five months he and his friends spent every day playing and having a wonderful time in the Land of Toys. Then one morning Pinocchio woke up and felt very strange. He put his hands on his head and felt his ears. They had grown long and hairy during the night! Soon he and all of his companions had turned into donkeys. Some were sold to farmers. Pinocchio was sold to a circus where he was beaten until he learned how to do tricks. He did very well until one day when he fell and hurt his leg.

Then he was sold for four cents for his skin. The buyer tied a stone around his neck, then a rope, and threw him into the sea to drown. Then his new master would skin him.

But Pinocchio was swallowed by an enormous shark. It was very dark in the belly of the fish, but Pinocchio could see a candle burning far away. He walked toward the light, and what did he find? I will give you a thousand guesses. He found a little old man with white hair sitting at a table eating fish. "Oh Father, dear Father. Have I found you at last? Now I shall never, never leave you again." And he and Geppetto walked down the shark's tongue, tickled it, and the shark gave a great sneeze. Out into the dark ocean they went, and Pinocchio put Geppetto on his back and swam to shore. Exhausted, Pinocchio carried Geppetto until they found a small hut, and only then did Pinocchio put his father down.

He went to a farm to ask for some milk for his father. But the farmer said that it cost money and if Pinocchio had no money he would get no milk. So Pinocchio offered to work for the milk, and he worked harder than he had ever worked in his life. The farmer was satisfied and gave him the milk. "I am so glad you came along. Until now, my donkey did the work, but he is dying." "Donkey?" said Pinocchio and ran to see. Yes, it was his old companion, Lamp-Wick. Pinocchio hugged the animal, and it died in his arms. For five months Pinocchio worked for the farmer so that he could make money to keep Geppetto from starving. At night he would study a schoolbook by candlelight. One night Pinocchio had a dream, and he saw the Fairy with the Blue Hair. She said, "Bravo, Pinocchio. I forgive you all your mischief. Boys who love and take care of their parents when they are old and sick deserve praise. Keep doing so well and you will be happy." When he awoke, he found that he was a real boy, and the little cottage was filled with beautiful furniture, clothes, flowers, and gold pieces. He ran to his father to find that Geppetto had grown years younger. "Oh, Pinocchio. This is all your doing," said Geppetto. "When bad boys become good and kind, they have the power of making their homes new with happiness."

And they lived happily ever after.

Checking Your Comprehension

Answer these questions in class.
1. How does Pinocchio meet Geppetto?
2. What happens to the Talking Cricket and why?
3. Why does the Fairy with the Blue Hair laugh at Pinocchio?
4. Why does Pinocchio turn into a donkey?

Be a Vocabulary Detective

Working in pairs, look for hints and guess the vocabulary from the context clues. Then fill in the blanks with the correct answers.

Clue 1

Geppetto is a *wood-carver*, and he can take a log and make a *marionette*.

1. *Carve* means_____ (v).
   a) to cut   b) to saw   c) to burn

2. A *marionette* is _____ (n).
   a) a table   b) a piece of wood   c) a puppet

Clue 2

Pinocchio kills the Talking *Cricket* when the Cricket warns Pinocchio that his life will be full of *grief* and *woe*.

3. A *cricket* is _____ (n).
   a) an insect that sings   b) a parrot   c) a dog

4. *Grief* is _____ (n).
   a) happiness   b) sadness   c) fear

5. *Woe* is _____ (n).
   a) hunger   b) grief   c) thirst

Clue 3

When Pinocchio lies to the Fairy with Blue Hair his nose grows. Since he is made out of wood, she sends for a *woodpecker* to cut down his nose.

6. A *woodpecker* is _____ (n).
   a) a bird   b) a carpenter   c) an ogre

Clue 4

The Fox and the Cat are *swindlers* and they steal the gold pieces from Pinocchio.

7. *Swindle* means_____ (v).
   a) to steal by cheating   b) to play   c) to help

Clue 5

Pinocchio and Geppetto need to escape from the shark so they *tickle* his tongue to make him sneeze.

8. *Tickle* means _____ (v).
   a) to hit   b) to bite   c) to touch lightly

Questions for Discussion

First, reread the story carefully looking for the deeper meanings and reviewing the vocabulary. Then in groups of four discuss the following questions with your classmates. Be sure to tell what your native culture is.
1. What was your favorite sentence in this story and why?
2. Why did it take Pinocchio such a long time to learn his lesson?
3. What is the significance of the boys being turned into donkeys?

Putting All the Pieces Together

Look at the puzzles on page 18 and page 23. Find the pieces that fit this story and discuss what cultural values this story teaches American children.

Double-checking the Vocabulary

Fill in the crossword with the following vocabulary words: carve, marionette, cricket, woe, swindler, woodpecker, grief, tickle.

Across

1. to cut in order to make a special shape
2. a bird with a long beak that makes holes in trees to find insects
3. to touch a part of the body lightly, producing laughter or discomfort

Down

4. a person who cheats, who gets money unlawfully
5. a wooden puppet that is moved by strings or wires
6. great sadness, especially over loss of something one loves
7. a small brown insect that makes loud short noises by rubbing its leathery wings together
8. great sorrow

Writing

Think, *in English*, about the most similar story in your culture. Then, using the vocabulary words, write it, *in English*, in correct American form and as briefly as possible.

Speaking

Now, tell your story.

Chapter  9

Individualism and Independence

This above all—to thine own self be true,
And it must follow, as the night the day,
Thou canst not then be false to any man.
—Shakespeare, *Hamlet,* 1.3

If I am not for myself, who will be for me?
—Hillel, 60 B.C.

The Little Red Hen

Reading Readiness

A. With a partner look at this advice column. Do you agree or disagree with the columnist? Try to guess the names of the characters in the story and what the story will be about.

ASK EUGENIA

Dear Eugenia
  My husband and I have had a terrible argument and we need your advice. My mother-in-law came to visit us for three (long) weeks. She is in her sixties and quite healthy, but she is so lazy she doesn't lift a finger to help. After two weeks of cooking and cleaning and entertaining for her I had had enough. Last week I spent some time in the kitchen cooking my grandmother's very complicated seven layer chocolate cake recipe. When it was out of the oven, I invited my daughter and her friends to share it with me. My mother-in-law got up from her nap and came into the kitchen just as we had finished the last crumbs. She was furious that we hadn't saved her any, and the rest of her stay was quite unpleasant. My husband says I was selfish and owe her an apology. What do you think?

Nobody's servant, Rome, Ga.

Dear Nobody's servant
  You sound just like the Little Red Hen, and like her, you have every right to eat what you make. Your mother-in-law didn't help; she deserves nothing. You chose to make the cake; you can choose to invite those you want to share. Your husband needs to re-check his marriage license. He married you, and his loyalties should be 100% to you. Your mother-in-law was way out of line. You're lucky she only stayed three weeks.

B. Look at these questions and share your ideas with the class.
1. In your culture which is valued more, being independent or working together?
2. In your culture, what is valued more, working for the pleasure of work or working to put food on the table?

Background Notes

This is an old English story made popular in America in the first half of the twentieth century. It is a tale about a chicken who wants to make some bread. It will help you understand the vocabulary if you think carefully about how bread is made and try to decide exactly how a chicken would make bread if she could do so.

Reading Selection

Now read this story once, as quickly as possible, for the general idea. Try to guess the meanings of the words you don't understand by the context. You can under-line the words you don't know, but don't stop reading.

Once upon a time there was a little red hen who lived on a farm. One day she went out to the farmyard to scratch for seeds. First she dug up the dirt with her left foot; then she dug up the dirt with her right foot. Every time she scratched, she looked to see what she could find. At last she found a grain of wheat.

"Cluck, cluck!" said the Little Red Hen. "Ah, I have finally found a grain of wheat. I will plant it."

She called to the Duck.

"Please, Duck, will you help me plant this grain of wheat?"

"No," said the Duck, "I will not."

She called to the Goose.

"Please, Goose, will you help me plant this grain of wheat?"

"No," said the Goose, "I will not."

Then she went to the Cat, who was dozing in the warm sun.

"Cat, will you help me plant this grain of wheat?"

"No," said the Cat, "I will not."

She went to the Pig.

"Pig, will you help me plant this grain of wheat?"

"No," said the Pig, "I will not."

So the Little Red Hen had to plant it all by herself. She scratched a hole in the ground, put in the grain, and covered it with dirt.

The sun shone and the rain fell. The wheat grew up tall and straight. It was ready to be taken to the mill to be made into flour.

"Cluck, cluck!" called the Little Red Hen. "Who will help me carry the wheat to the mill?"

"Not I," said the Duck.

"Not I," said the Goose.

"Not I," said the Cat.

"Not I," said the Pig.

So the Little Red Hen plucked the wheat and carried it to the mill herself. The mill stood on a clear stream, quite far away. The Little Red Hen was all out of breath when she got there.

"Please, Miller, here is some wheat. Will you grind it into flour, so I can bake a loaf of bread?"

"Yes," said the miller, "I will."

A day came and a day went. The Little Red Hen walked to the mill. She got the flour, flung the bag on her back, and started off for home. Halfway there she had to rest. The flour was very heavy. But at last she got to the door of her little house.

"Cluck, cluck!" said the Little Red Hen, "Who will help me make the dough?"

"Not I," said the Duck.

"Not I," said the Goose.

"Not I," said the Cat.

"Not I," said the Pig.

So the Little Red Hen had to make it all by herself. She put on a large white apron. Then she took down a bowl and put in the flour, some water, some salt, and some yeast and mixed it all together. Soon the dough was ready to go into the oven.

"Cluck, cluck!" called the Little Red Hen. "Who will help me bake the dough?"

"Not I," said the Duck.

"Not I," said the Goose.

"Not I," said the Cat.

"Not I," said the Pig.

So the Little Red Hen had to bake it all by herself.

After the sweet brown loaf had been taken from the oven, she placed it on the table to cool.

"Now, who will help me eat the bread?" she cried.

"I will," said the Duck.

"I will," said the Goose.

"I will," said the Cat.

"I will," said the Pig.

But the Little Red Hen said, "No, you cannot have any. You did not help me, so I will eat it all by myself."

Checking Your Comprehension

Answer these questions in class.

1. Does the Little Red Hen plan to make the bread because she is hungry?
2. Who helps the Little Red Hen?
3. How do the Duck, Goose, Cat, and Pig feel at the end of the story?
4. How does the Little Red Hen feel at the end of the story?

Be a Vocabulary Detective

Working in pairs, look for hints and guess the vocabulary from the context clues. Then fill in the blanks with the correct answers.

Clue 1

The Little Red Hen is a chicken. Think about how chickens act, walk, work, etc. What do they eat? How do they find their food? The Little Red Hen was *scratching* the ground looking for *seeds*.

1. *Scratch* means _____ (v).
   a) to itch   b) to eat   c) to rub

2. *Seeds* are_____ (n).
   a) vegetables   b) small grains   c) fruit

Clue 2

This a story about animals. Think about the Cat. There's only one thing cats do in the warm sun, isn't there? The Cat is *dozing* in the warm sun. (Do you doze in class?)

3. *Doze* means _____ (v).
   a) to dance   b) to smile   c) to sleep

Clue 3

The Little Red Hen wants to make some bread. How do you make bread? Well, first she had to *plant* the *grain*. To do that she *dug* the ground with her feet. When the wheat was ready, she *plucked* it.

4. *Plant* means _____ (v).
   a) to eat   b) to put in the ground   c) to harvest

5. A *grain* is_____ (n).
   a) a seed   b) a liquid   c) blue

6. *Dig* means _____ (v).
   a) to fill   b) to empty   c) to clean

7. *Pluck* means _____ (v).
   a) to pull   b) to steal   c) to cook

Clue 4

The Little Red Hen must take the wheat to a *mill* where the miller will *grind* it into flour. Of course, the mill is on a clear *stream*.

8. A *mill* is _____ (n).
   a) a place that makes flour   b) a movie theater   c) a grocery store

9. *Grind* means _____ (v).
   a) to crush   b) to erase   c) to clean

10. A *stream* is _____ (n).
   a) an ocean   b) the seashore   c) a very small river

Clue 5

The mill is very far away, and the bag of wheat is very heavy. No wonder the Little Red Hen is *out of breath*.

11. To be *out of breath* means _____ (idiom).
    a) to be hungry   b) to have a sore neck   c) to have trouble breathing

Clue 6

How would a chicken carry a heavy bag of flour? Probably on her back. How would she get it there? Chickens don't have arms or hands, only beaks. The Little Red Hen *flung* the flour on her back.

12. *Fling* (present tense of *flung*) means _____ (v).
    a) to throw   b) to hold   c) to tie

Clue 7

Do you know how to make bread? You need some flour, some water, and some salt. But that will make only crackers. The Little Red Hen put in the *yeast* to make the bread rise.

13. *Yeast* is _____ (n).
    a) a seed   b) a living organism   c) some pepper

Clue 8

Then the *dough* was ready to go into the oven. What would happen if you took a little piece of that dough, rolled it into the shape of a nut, and fried it? *(Hint:* it tastes good with coffee at breakfast.)

14. *Dough* means _____ (n).
    a) raw bread   b) uncooked crackers   c) a bowl

Questions for Discussion

First, reread the story carefully looking for the deeper meanings and reviewing the vocabulary. Then in groups of four discuss the following questions with your classmates. Be sure to tell what your native culture is.
1. What was your favorite sentence in this story and why?
2. Does the Little Red Hen need the bread for her food or does the Little Red Hen want the bread for her pleasure?
3. Are the other farm animals punished because they didn't help or are the other farm animals just disappointed because they don't get a treat?

Putting All the Pieces Together

Look at the puzzles on page 18 and page 23. Find the pieces that fit this story and discuss what cultural values this folktale teaches American children.

Double-checking the Vocabulary

Look at the definitions and cross out the words in the list that match. Then, looking at the words that remain, read from left to right, top to bottom, and find the answer to the question, "What does the Little Red Hen say to her children?"

a. to put something in the ground so it will grow
b. the small beginnings of life
c. opposite of itch
d. to make a hole in the ground
e. the building where flour is made
f. the seed from the wheat plant, a grass like rice, oats, and corn
g. unbaked mixture of water, flour, yeast, and salt
h. to sleep very lightly
i. to pull something out quickly and with force
j. a small river
k. having trouble breathing
l. to throw something quickly and with force
m. to make something into small pieces from a large whole
n. a living organism that makes bread rise and wine ferment

you	scratch	plant	pluck	fling
grind	can	out of breath	only	doze
seed	depend	grain	mill	stream
on	dig	yeast	dough	yourself

Writing

Think, *in English*, about the most similar story in your culture. Then, using the vocabulary words, write it, *in English*, in correct American form and as briefly as possible.

Speaking

Now, tell your story.

Charlotte's Web

Reading Readiness

A. With a partner look at this book cover. Describe what you see. Try to guess the names of the characters in the story and what the story will be about.

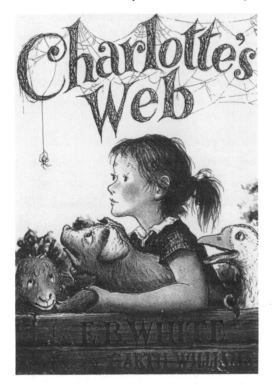

B. Look at these questions and share your ideas with the class.
   1. When you were a child did you ever question what your father (or mother) was doing? Did you ever disagree and argue with them? Describe what happened.
   2. Did you ever have a pet when you were a child? What kind of pet?

Background Notes

This is the first chapter (entitled "Before Breakfast") from a very beloved children's classic written by E. B. White in 1952. You might want to read the whole book. There is also a video, a musical cartoon, made in 1972. You might want to see it after you read the book. E. B. White wrote two other children's books, *Stuart Little* and *The Trumpet of the Swan*, which you might also want to read.

Reading Selection

Now read this story once, as quickly as possible, for the general idea. Try to guess the meanings of the words you don't understand by the context. You can underline the words you don't know, but don't stop reading.

"Where's Papa going with that ax?" said Fern to her mother as they were setting the table for breakfast.

"Out to the hoghouse," replied Mrs. Arable. "Some pigs were born last night."

"I don't see why he needs an ax," continued Fern, who was only eight.

"Well," said her mother, "one of the pigs is a runt. It's very small and weak, and it will never amount to anything. So your father has decided to do away with it."

"Do *away* with it?" shrieked Fern. "You mean kill it? Just because it's smaller than the others?"

Mrs. Arable put a pitcher of cream on the table. "Don't yell, Fern!" she said. "Your father is right. The pig would probably die anyway."

Fern pushed a chair out of the way and ran outdoors. The grass was wet and the earth smelled of springtime. Fern's sneakers were sopping by the time she caught up with her father.

"Please don't kill it!" she sobbed. "It's unfair."

Mr. Arable stopped walking.

"Fern," he said gently, "you will have to learn to control yourself."

"Control myself?" yelled Fern. "This is a matter of life and death, and you talk about *controlling* myself." Tears ran down her cheeks and she took hold of the ax and tried to pull it out of her father's hand.

"Fern," said Mr. Arable, "I know more about raising a litter of pigs than you do. A weakling makes trouble. Now run along!"

"But it's unfair," cried Fern. "The pig couldn't help being born small, could it? If I had been very small at birth, would you have killed *me?*"

Mr. Arable smiled. "Certainly not," he said, looking down at his daughter with love. "But this is different. A little girl is one thing, a little runty pig is another."

"I see no difference," replied Fern, still hanging on to the ax. "This is the most terrible case of injustice I ever heard of."

A queer look came over John Arable's face. He seemed almost ready to cry himself.

"All right," he said. "You go back to the house and I will bring the runt when I come in. I'll let you start it on a bottle, like a baby. Then you'll see what trouble a pig can be."

When Mr. Arable returned to the house half an hour later, he carried a carton under his arms. Fern was upstairs changing her sneakers. The kitchen table was set for breakfast, and the room smelled of coffee, bacon, damp plaster, and wood smoke from the stove.

"Put it on her chair!" said Mrs. Arable. Mr. Arable set the carton down at Fern's place. Then he walked to the sink and washed his hands and dried them on the roller towel.

Fern came slowly down the stairs. Her eyes were red from crying. As she approached her chair, the carton wobbled, and there was a scratching noise. Fern looked at her father. Then she lifted the lid of the carton. There, inside, looking up at her, was the newborn pig. It was a white one. The morning light shone through its ears, turning them pink.

"He's yours," said Mr. Arable. "Saved from an untimely death. And may the good Lord forgive me for this foolishness."

Fern couldn't take her eyes off the tiny pig. "Oh," she whispered. "Oh, look at him! He's absolutely perfect."

She closed the carton carefully. First she kissed her father, then she kissed her mother. Then she opened the lid again, lifted the pig out, and held it against her cheek. At this moment her brother Avery came into the room. Avery was ten. He was heavily armed—an air rifle in one hand, a wooden dagger in the other.

"What's that?" he demanded. "What's Fern got?"

"She's got a guest for breakfast," said Mrs. Arable. "Wash your hands and face, Avery!"

"Let's see it!" said Avery, setting his gun down. "You call that miserable thing a pig? That's a *fine* specimen of a pig—it's no bigger than a white rat."

"Wash up and eat your breakfast, Avery!" said his mother. "The school bus will be along in half an hour."

"Can I have a pig, too, Pop?" asked Avery.

"No, I only distribute pigs to early risers," said Mr. Arable. "Fern was up at daylight, trying to rid the world of injustice. As a result, she now has a pig. A small one, to be sure, but nevertheless a pig. It just goes to show what can happen if a person gets out of bed promptly. Let's eat!"

But Fern couldn't eat until her pig had had a drink of milk. Mrs. Arable found a baby's nursing bottle and a rubber nipple. She poured warm milk into the bottle, fitted the nipple over the top, and handed it to Fern. "Give him his breakfast!" she said.

A minute later, Fern was seated on the floor in the corner of the kitchen with her infant between her knees, teaching it to suck from the bottle. The pig, although tiny, had a good appetite and caught on quickly.

The school bus honked from the road.

"Run!" commanded Mrs. Arable, taking the pig from Fern and slipping a doughnut into her hand. Avery grabbed his gun and another doughnut.

The children ran out to the road and climbed into the bus. Fern took no notice of the others in the bus. She just sat and stared out of the window, thinking what a blissful world it was and how lucky she was to have entire charge of a pig. By the time the bus reached school, Fern had named her pet, selecting the most beautiful name she could think of.

"Its name is Wilbur," she whispered to herself.

She was still thinking about the pig when the teacher said: "Fern, what is the capital of Pennsylvania?"

"Wilbur," replied Fern, dreamily. The pupils giggled. Fern blushed.

Checking Your Comprehension

Answer these questions in class.
1. What is Fern doing at the start of the story?
2. Why is she so upset when her mother tells her what her father plans to do?
3. Why does Mr. Arable decide to let Fern raise the pig?
4. Whom does Fern kiss, in what order, and why?

Be a Vocabulary Detective

Working in pairs, look for hints and guess the vocabulary from the context clues. Then fill in the blanks with the correct answers.

Clue 1

Mr. Arable is a farmer, and a *litter* of pigs has just been born. One is too small and weak. Mr. Arable goes to the *hoghouse* with an *ax* to kill the baby pig that is a *runt*.

1. A *litter* is _____ (n).
    a) mail   b) not doing anything   c) baby animals born together

2. A *hoghouse* is _____ (n).
    a) where pigs live   b) a dirty house   c) a restaurant

3. An *ax* is_____ (n).
    a) a tool   b) an animal   c) a gun

4. A *runt* is _____ (n).
    a) a giant   b) an unusually small animal   c) a toy

Clue 2

It is an early morning in the springtime, and the grass is extremely wet. As Fern runs after her father her *sneakers* become *sopping*.

5. *Sneakers* are _____ (n).
    a) socks   b) pants   c) tennis shoes

6. *Sopping* is _____ (adj).
    a) extremely wet   b) dirty   c) torn

Clue 3

Mr. Arable is so proud of his daughter's concern for freedom, equality, and justice that a *queer* look comes over his face and he almost starts to cry.

7. *Queer* means _____ (adj).
    a) normal   b) very strange   c) happy

Clue 4

The carton *wobbles* because the pig is inside. Fern removes the pig, and Avery, who has come into the room carrying a toy gun and a toy *dagger*, makes fun of it by saying, "That's a fine *specimen* of a pig."

8. *Wobble* means _____ (v).
    a) to move   b) to make noise   c) to fall

9. A *dagger* is _____ (n).
    a) a small stick   b) a small gun   c) a small knife

10. A *specimen* is _____ (n).
   a) a pet   b) a toy   c) an example

Clue 5

Mrs. Arable knew that the pig had just been born and needed to suck milk like a baby, so she put a *nipple* on the baby bottle and gave it to Fern.

11. A *nipple* is _____ (n).
   a) something used for sucking   b) something used for feeding
   c) something used for cleaning

Clue 6

Fern is so extremely happy with her pig that she doesn't pay attention in school. She feels that it is a *blissful* world. When she makes a mistake, all the children *giggle* at Fern. Fern is so embarrassed she *blushes*.

12. *Blissful* means _____ (adj).
   a) extremely unhappy   b) extremely happy   c) extremely frightened

13. *Giggle* means _____ (v).
   a) to laugh   b) to cry   c) to cough

14. *Blush* means _____ (v).
   a) to look sad   b) to turn red   c) to smile

Questions for Discussion

First, reread the story carefully, looking for the deeper meanings and reviewing the vocabulary. Then in groups of four discuss the following questions with your classmates. Be sure to tell what your native culture is.
1. What was your favorite sentence in this story and why?
2. Is Fern a well-behaved child or a badly behaved child? Give several examples from the story to prove your point.
3. Were you surprised that Fern's father was "looking down at his daughter with love" instead of looking down in anger because she disagreed with him? If so, explain why.

Putting All the Pieces Together

Look at the puzzles on page 18 and page 23. Find the pieces that fit this story and discuss what cultural values this story teaches American children.

Double-checking the Vocabulary

Fill in the crossword with the following vocabulary words: ax, hoghouse, runt, sneakers, sopping, litter, queer, wobble, dagger, specimen, nipple, blissful, giggle, blush, Rx.

Across

1. extremely wet
2. the place on the farm where the pigs live
3. an example
4. very strange

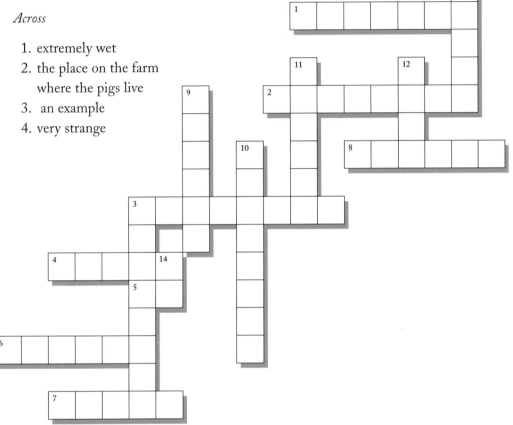

Down

5. a chopping tool with a long wooden handle and a heavy metal blade
6. a piece of rubber on a bottle with a hole for sucking, shaped like the end of a breast
7. to turn red in the face from embarrassment or shame
8. a group of young animals born at the same time to one mother

3. cloth shoes with rubber soles
9. a short pointed knife used as a weapon
10. feeling complete happiness, as if one were in heaven
11. to move unevenly
12. a small, weak animal or person
13. a light laugh
14. another name for a prescription for medicine a doctor writes

Writing

Think, *in English*, about the most similar story in your culture. Then, using the vocabulary words, write it, *in English*, in correct American form and as briefly as possible.

Speaking

Now, tell your story.

Davy Crockett

Reading Readiness

A. With a partner look at this advertisement. Describe what you see. Try to guess the names of the characters in the story and what the story will be about.

B. Look at these questions and share your ideas with the class.

   1. Name a famous hero (who really lived) in your culture. Describe the main characteristics of that person.

   2. Do people go hunting in your culture? What is the animal they usually look for?

Background Notes

This story is from an autobiography called *The Life of Colonel David Crockett, Written by Himself.* Davy Crockett was an all-American hero who lived from 1786 to 1836 when the United States was a very young country. Many think that the autobiography was really dictated because Davy had no formal education. Some think he couldn't read or write at all, but he was a very clever man with a great sense of humor. He was very famous for his bravery and his ability to shoot his rifle, both of which he demonstrated in war battles (1813–14). His skill at shooting his rifle also showed when he was hunting bears and raccoons. He was elected to the government of the new state of Tennessee two times and then to the U.S. Congress twice. He died in the famous Battle of the Alamo in Texas in 1836 during the Mexican-American War. What you will now read was originally written in a dialect that imitated the way Davy Crockett used to speak. You might be surprised at how much he exaggerates and boasts in this story, but that was an important part of the new America where people felt that everything was bigger and better and newer. Davy Crockett was a real folk hero. Heroes achieve what the common person dreams of achieving. In the 1800s the American hero was a plain common man who could perform the impossible. Davy Crockett did exactly that, and each time someone repeated a story about Davy, he got bigger and bigger than life. Why, he could even talk to animals!

Reading Selection

Now read this story once, as quickly as possible, for the general idea. Try to guess the meanings of the words you don't understand by the context. You can underline the words you don't know, but don't stop reading.

Well, they asked me how I got into politics, as I was considered an ignorant backwoods bear hunter. When I first decided to run for the Tennessee legislature, I stood in front of the crowds and tried to say something about the government, but no words came out. There the people stood, listening all the while, and there was nothing in my mouth. So I told them about this fellow who was shaking an enormous bottle and a friend asked him what he was doing. The fellow replied that there had been some cider in that bottle a few days before, and he was trying to see if there was any left, and if there was he couldn't get it out. So, I told them I was just like that man; I had a little bit of a political speech in me but I believe I couldn't get it out. They all roared with a mighty laugh, and then I told them I was a screamer and had the biggest horse, the prettiest sister, and the surest rifle in the district. My father could whip any man in Tennessee and I can whip my father. I can outspeak any man, run faster, dive deeper, stay longer underwater, than anyone. I can outstare any mountain lion and carry a steamboat on my back. I can walk like an ox, run like a fox, swim like a fish, yell like an Indian, fight like a devil, and make love like a mad bull. And that's how I got elected to the government.

Well, right after the election I was feeling real hungry and had a craving for raccoon stew. Now, almost everybody who knows the forest understands perfectly well that Davy Crockett never loses his gunpowder, having been brought up to believe that it is a sin to throw away ammunition. Waste not, want not was my education. So there I was out in the forest and had just got to the place they call the Great Gap and I saw a raccoon sitting up all alone in a tree. I put my trusted rifle, who I called Brown Betty, to my shoulder and was just going to put some lead between the shoulders of that raccoon when he lifted one paw and he said to me, "Is your name Davy Crockett?"

"Well," I said to him, "You are right for once, yes, my name is Davy Crockett."

"Then," he said, "you needn't trouble yourself with the shooting for I might as well come on right down without another word." And the creature walked right down from the tree because he considered himself already dead.

I stooped down and patted him on the head and said, "I hope I may be shot myself before I hurt a hair of your head for I have never received such a compliment in my entire life."

"Well, you're quite welcome," said the raccoon. "So I guess I might as well just walk off for the present. I don't doubt your word a bit, but the famous Davy Crockett might just change his mind."

Now that was one clever raccoon, and this Davy Crockett went hungry that night.

Checking Your Comprehension

Answer these questions in class.
1. Why does Davy compare himself to the man with the empty cider bottle?
2. Why do you think Davy got elected?
3. Why did the raccoon come down from the tree instead of running away?

Be a Vocabulary Detective

Working in pairs, look for hints and guess the vocabulary from the context clues. Then fill in the blanks with the correct answers.

Clue 1

Davy never lived in a city but grew up deep in the woods. Although he traveled all over the new country and fought hard in the war, some people thought he was just a *backwoods* bear hunter. They also thought Davy was *ignorant* because he had no formal education in school.

1. *Backwoods* means _____ (adj).
   a) city   b) town   c) far from society

2. *Ignorant* means_____ (adj).
   a) smart   b) stupid   c) poor

Clue 2

Davy had a *craving* for raccoon stew. He wanted to shoot the raccoon, so he put the *ammunition* in the rifle. It was made out of *lead*.

3. *Crave* means_____ (v).
   a) to desire   b) to dislike   c) to fear

4. *Ammunition* is _____ (n).
   a) arrows   b) bullets   c) stones

5. *Lead* is _____ (n).
   a) a heavy metal   b) plastic   c) wood

Clue 3

People say that *raccoons* look like robbers. Davy's raccoon was a smart *creature*. When the little raccoon raised its *paw* and came down the tree, Davy wanted to pat it, but he was so tall he had to *stoop down* to reach it.

6. A *raccoon* is _____ (n).
   a) a small animal   b) a thief   c) a dinner

7. A *creature* is _____ (n).
   a) an animal   b) a man   c) a child

8. A *paw* is _____ (n).
   a) a hand   b) a mouth   c) a father

9. *Stoop down* means_____ (v).
   a) to stand tall   b) to bend down   c) to sit

Clue 4

Davy got into politics by running in an election for the Tennessee *legislature*. He wanted to get elected to the state government, so he entertained the people. And the crowd of people *roared* with laughter.

10. The *legislature* is _____ (n).
     a) part of the government   b) part of the kingdom
     c) part of a dictatorship

11. To *roar* means to make a sound like_____ (v).
     a) a lion   b) a raccoon   c) a bird

Clue 5

Davy was exaggerating a lot because that's what the people liked, so he said he could *whip* his father.
12. *Whip* is _____(v).
     a) to hug   b) to defeat   c) to carry

Questions for Discussion

First, reread the story carefully looking for the deeper meanings and reviewing the vocabulary. Then in groups of four discuss the following questions with your classmates. Be sure to tell what your native culture is.
1. What was your favorite sentence in this story and why?
2. List the characteristics of Davy Crockett that made him an American hero.
3. Were you surprised that the people liked the boasting and exaggeration of Davy Crockett? Would a hero of your culture have the same qualities? Would your culture consider Davy Crockett a liar?

Putting All the Pieces Together

Look at the puzzles on page 18 and page 23. Find the pieces that fit this story and discuss what cultural values this hero tale teaches American children.

Double-checking the Vocabulary

Look at the definitions and cross out the words in the list that match. Then, looking at the words that remain, read from left to right, top to bottom, and find the answer to the question, "How did the raccoon save his life?"

a. the hand or foot of an animal
b. lacking knowledge
c. an animal of any kind
d. bullets, explosives, things fired from a weapon
e. to desire intensely
f. a soft, heavy metal
g. the part of the government that has the power to make and change laws
h. to bend over
i. to make a deep, loud, continuing sound, like a lion
j. a small meat-eating North American animal with black fur over its eyes like a mask
k. to defeat
l. uncleared land far away from town

ignorant	he	backwoods	legislature	roar
whip	crave	was	raccoon	ammunition
lead	clever	paw	creature	stoop down

Writing

Think, *in English*, about the most similar story in your culture. Then, using the vocabulary words, write it, *in English*, in correct American form and as briefly as possible.

Speaking

Now, tell your story.

Paul Bunyan

Reading Readiness

A. With a partner look at this political cartoon. Describe what you see. Try to guess the names of the characters in the story and what the story will be about.

America Needs Paul Bunyan Now!

B. Look at these questions and share your ideas with the class.
   1. Have you ever exaggerated a story to make it bigger than reality?
   2. Do you have any stories in your culture about a hero who is larger than life?

Background Notes

This is an American tall tale that probably originated from the stories about a French-Canadian lumberjack named Paul Bunyon, who lived in Canada in the 1830s. By 1860, the story had crossed the border to the United States, the *o* had been exchanged for an *a,* and Paul Bunyan had become a legendary American hero. At night the lumberjacks would sit around the campfire and have storytelling contests to see who could add the most exaggerated details to the story of this great American. At each telling the stories grew larger and larger. In 1914, some of the stories were published.

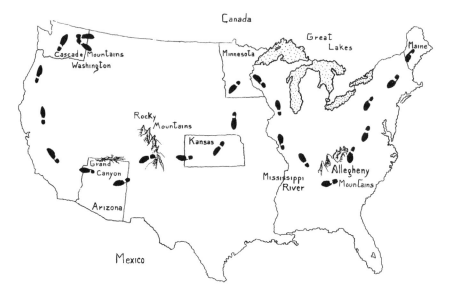

Reading Selection

Now read this story once, as quickly as possible, for the general idea. Try to guess the meanings of the words you don't understand by the context. You can underline the words you don't know, but don't stop reading.

One December, a long time ago, when America was a very new country and the land was not yet fully formed, a very unique baby was born in Maine to Mr. and Mrs. Bunyan. They named their son Paul and were very surprised at his size. He grew quite rapidly, and at two weeks he weighed more than 100 pounds. He also had grown a big, bushy, black beard that his mother had to comb with a pine tree. Paul was a good baby, but he needed to eat enormous amounts of food. It cost his parents an arm and a leg to feed him.

When Paul started crawling at nine months the neighbors started to complain. They felt like there was a constant earthquake in the town. His parents loved him very much, but eventually they were forced to take their 500-pound, 18-month-old toddler to a cave in the Maine Woods quite far away from any civilization. With tears in their eyes, they left their baby. The poor baby cried so hard for thirty days and thirty nights that a whole river was formed. When the hungry Paul saw that river he stopped crying and started fishing, and there he lived all alone for the first twenty years of his life. Paul towered above the tallest trees, and he could cross 24 towns at one step when he was in a hurry. One day he sneezed, and it caused a landslide on Pike's Peak.

On his twenty-first birthday there was a storm that had never been seen before. It snowed, and the snow was blue. Paul went for a walk in the woods and was overjoyed to see everything covered in blue. Suddenly he heard a sound, "Maaa-maa." like a baby crying for its parents. "Where are you, baby?" he cried, and he suddenly saw a tail, and two horns sticking out of the snow. He pulled on the tail, and out came a baby ox, as blue as the snow and of enormous size. Paul took the frozen baby home and fell asleep with the baby in his arms. In the morning Paul was delighted to find that the ox was alive and was kissing him with her warm tongue. He had found a friend, and he named her Babe. Babe grew just as fast as Paul Bunyan had grown. Why if Paul closed his eyes, that baby would be one foot taller when Paul opened his eyes! When Babe the Blue Ox was fully grown she measured 42 ax handles and could pull anything that needed to be pulled.

One night Paul had a dream and saw the words *real America* burning into a forest and clearing the land. He heard a whisper in the air that said, "Work. Take advantage of your opportunity." He heard a louder cry, "Work, work, work," and realized that clearing the forest and making logs would be his lifework.

Well, at that time America was filled with dark green forests, and Paul knew from his dream that the pioneers needed wood to build their houses and towns. So one day Paul Bunyan invented logging. He took his big ax and chopped down the trees. Then he put the trees on Babe's back and they walked to the river. "It's too crooked," he said. He tied a rope to Babe and the other end of the rope to the river and said, "Pull," and Babe pulled and made the river straight. They sent the logs to the sawmill in Minnesota and then walked through the North Woods cutting and clearing the forests. Babe was so thirsty that Paul made the Great Lakes as reservoirs for Babe's drinking water. He piled up the Allegheny Mountains on one side and the Rocky Mountains on the other side when he dug a channel for the Mississippi River. He made Kansas flat when he tied Babe to the ground and turned it over to make good land for growing corn. Then Paul and Babe went off to Arizona dragging their tools behind them. Paul didn't know it, but dragging those tools made the Grand Canyon.

When Paul Bunyan was thirty years old he opened up a logging camp and only allowed men over 10 feet tall to apply for the jobs. He had over 1,000 men working for him, and he ruled over the woods from the Winter of the Blue Snow until the Spring That the Rain Came from China. That year it rained for forty days and forty nights. When the rain was over Paul stood on the Cascade Mountains in Washington and looked at America. The rain had washed away the forests, and he could see only flat prairies. He looked at his lumberjacks, and they had become ordinary men again. Then Paul saw that his lifework had ended. He and Babe disappeared into the forest. Now all that's left of Paul are the stories that are told about him, and those stories will never disappear.

Checking Your Comprehension

Answer these questions in class.
1. Why did Mr. and Mrs. Bunyan leave Paul in a cave?
2. Why does Paul name his blue ox Babe?
3. According to the tale, where do the Allegheny and Rocky Mountains come from?
4. Why do Paul and Babe disappear into the forest after the Spring That the Rain Came from China?

Be a Vocabulary Detective

Working in pairs, look for hints and guess the vocabulary from the context clues. Then fill in the blanks with the correct answers.

Clue 1

Paul was a *unique* baby, the largest ever born in the world. Like most babies, he started *crawling* when he was nine months old. But unlike most babies, Paul made so much noise the neighbors complained. It *cost* his parents *an arm and a leg* to feed him. So when Paul was a *toddler,* his parents left him in the Maine Woods. As an adult, he *towered* over the trees and when Paul sneezed, he caused a *landslide.*

1. *Unique* means _____ (adj).
   a) ordinary   b) playful   c) one of a kind

2. *Crawl* means_____ (v).
   a) to run   b) to move on hands and knees   a) to walk

3. A *toddler* is _____ (n).
   a) 6 months old   b)18 months old   c) 36 months old

4. *To cost an arm and a leg* is _____ (idiom).
   a) to be cheap   b) to be expensive   c) to be on sale

5. *Tower* means _____ (v).
   a) to be taller   b) to be shorter   c) to be a building

6. A *landslide* is _____ (n).
   a) snow falling down a hill   b) rocks falling down a hill
   c) water falling down a hill

Clue 2

Paul chose as his lifework to be a *lumberjack* cutting down the forests. He opened
a *logging camp* and hired *loggers* to cut the trees into *logs*.

7. A *lumberjack* is _____ (n).
   a) a fisherman   b) a tree-cutter   c) a salesperson

8. A *logging camp* is _____ (n).
   a) in the forest   b) in the desert   c) at the park

9. *A logger* is _____ (n).
   a) a tree cutter   b) a butcher   c) a sailor

10. A *log* is_____ (n).
    a) metal   b) plastic   c) wood

Clue 3

Paul found a baby animal in the snow. At first he thought it was a cow, but she
was an *ox*. He named her Babe, and she grew to be 42 *ax handles* tall. In case she
got thirsty, Paul made the Great Lakes as a *reservoir* for Babe.

11. An *ox* is _____ (n).
    a) a horse   b) the uncle of the cow   c) a donkey

12. An *ax handle* means _____ (idiom).
    a) 2H feet   b) a tree   c) something to eat

13. A *reservoir* is _____ (n).
    a) storage for water   b) a bathtub   c) a sea

Clue 4

The river was *crooked*, so Paul and Babe tried to make it straight so that it would be easy to send the lumber to the mill.

14. *Crooked* is _____ (adj).
    a) high   b) bent   c) full

Questions for Discussion

First, reread the story carefully looking for the deeper meanings and reviewing the vocabulary. Then in groups of four discuss the following questions with your classmates. Be sure to tell what your native culture is.
1. What was your favorite sentence in this story and why?
2. Was it an important part of the story for Paul to meet Babe the Blue Ox?
3. What is the significance of Paul's dream?
4. What parts of the story did you believe? What parts did you doubt?

Putting All the Pieces Together

Look at the puzzles on page 18 and page 23. Find the pieces that fit this story and discuss what cultural values this tall tale teaches American children.

Double-checking the Vocabulary

Fill in the crossword with the following vocabulary words: lumberjack, unique, cost an arm and a leg, crawl, toddler, to tower, landslide, ox, ax handles, log, logger, logging camp, crooked, reservoir. You will also need the words *six, ten,* and *to.*

Across

1. to move on the hands and knees
2. to be extremely expensive
3. large work animal of the cattle family, usually a male cow that cannot breed
4. a thick piece of wood from a tree
5. a sudden fall of earth or rocks down a hill or mountain
6. a person who cuts down trees for wood
7. how many fingers do you have?
8. the number after five
9. a synonym for lumberjack

Down

10. place where loggers live, eat, and sleep
11. a preposition
12. a way of measuring by using the handle of an ax, which is usually two and a half feet long
13. to be taller than anyone else
14. a child who has just learned to walk
15. not straight
16. one of a kind
17. a place where liquid is stored

Writing

Think, *in English*, about the most similar story in your culture. Then, using the vocabulary words, write it, *in English*, in correct American form and as briefly as possible.

Speaking

Now, tell your story.

Johnny Appleseed

Reading Readiness

A. With a partner look at this advertisement. Describe what you see. Try to guess the names of the characters in the story and what the story will be about.

B. Look at these questions and share your ideas with the class.
1. Can you think of a hero in your country, a real person whose story gets more exciting with each telling? Share that story with your neighbor.
2. Is there a special food in your country that has a historical meaning? What is this food, and why does it have this meaning?

Background Notes

You probably eat apples. Have you ever stopped to wonder where they come from? They are not native to North America, yet when we talk about the United States, we often talk about "apple pie." Well, here is a story about a real man who lived in the early 1800s in the United States. He was a very strange man who loved planting apple trees.

Reading Selection

Now read this story once, as quickly as possible, for the general idea. Try to guess the meanings of the words you don't understand by the context. You can underline the words you don't know, but don't stop reading.

Once there was a pioneer named John Chapman. He was born in Boston, Massachusetts, in 1775 and, after the American Revolution, moved with his brother Nathaniel to a farm in the hills of western Pennsylvania. John had always been a dreamer and very eccentric. He could never sit still. He was extremely religious, always reading the Bible and telling his friends about the long conversations he had with the angels. So when, at the age of 25, he told his brother that he had decided to become a missionary, his brother was not surprised. But Johnny said that he was not going to become an ordinary missionary. No, he would become an "apple missionary." He had had a dream in which an angel came to him to show him how to help the brave new pioneers make a new life in their vast new land. He told Nathaniel that the angel had shown him apple orchards shining throughout the wilderness of the new American territory.

Johnny then gathered apple seeds from all the cider mills around western Pennsylvania. He dried the seeds in the sun, packed them into deerskin sacks, and in 1806 traveled in a canoe down the Ohio River. He would call out to the settlers to "take God's jewels," plant the seeds, and then harvest the fruit. When Johnny ran out of seeds, he would walk back to Pennsylvania to get more.

Johnny was an extremely strange-looking man, small yet strong, with bright black eyes. He always wore nothing but a big coffee sack with openings cut out for his head, arms, and legs. He wore a tin pot on his head, and he would cook his breakfast cereal in his hat! He never wore shoes. He would walk barefoot through forests filled with rattlesnakes and through the snows of winter. People would give him nice clothes and shoes, but he would always give those to others who were more needy. The pioneers would always greet him with love and respect and invite him into their homes. Johnny would only sit down at dinner if there were children present, and he always spent the night outside or sometimes in barns.

The Native Americans regarded him as a great healer and respected his powers, for he would often thrust hot pins into his body to show how strong he was. He was a vegetarian and ate only the nuts and berries that he found growing wild. He believed it was a sin to kill any living creature, and he often would buy animals he thought were being abused and then give them away to whoever would care for them. One day he felt something bite his foot and threw down his shovel on top of a rattlesnake, killing it. He wept and said, "Poor fellow, he only just touched me, when I, in the heat of my ungodly passion, killed him and went away." One cold night he lit a fire, and, noticing how many moths and mosquitoes were burning in the fire, he immediately put the fire out. "God forbid that I should build a fire for my comfort which should be the means of destroying any of God's creatures."

For forty years Johnny Appleseed walked all over the new American territory planting apple trees, greeting the new pioneers with his Bible and saying "I've come to light a candle of understanding. I've got news fresh from heaven."

One summer day in 1847, Johnny Appleseed, at the age of 72, stopped to rest at a farm in Indiana. As usual, he refused the offer to come in to eat or sleep. He lay down in the barn, dreaming of his animals and his apple trees, and Johnny never woke up from that last dream. The doctor who was called said he had never seen such a glow of light on a dying man's face.

Today, every time an American bites an apple he or she is saying thank you to Johnny Appleseed, that independent, free spirit who chose to do what made him happy.

Checking Your Comprehension

Answer these questions in class.

1. Why did Johnny Appleseed plant apples?
2. Where did Johnny Appleseed live?
3. Why was Johnny a vegetarian?

Be a Vocabulary Detective

Working in pairs, look for hints and guess the vocabulary from the context clues. Then fill in the blanks with the correct answers.

Clue 1

Some might say that Johnny Appleseed was crazy. Definitely he was *eccentric*. Johnny always carried a Bible and spread the word of God by planting apples. He was a *missionary* for apples.

1. *Eccentric* means _____ (adj).
   a) ordinary   b) strange   c) old

2. A *missionary* is_____ (n).
   a) a doctor   b) a farmer   c) a religious teacher

Clue 2

Johnny lived when America was a *vast* unpopulated country from the Atlantic Ocean to the Pacific Ocean. He helped the *pioneers* establish the enormous empty land as the people moved from the cities into the *wilderness*.

3. *Vast* means _____ (adj).
   a) small   b) enormous   c) full

4. A *pioneer* is_____ (n).
   a) a settler   b) a planter   c) a cowboy

5. A *wilderness* is _____ (n).
   a) a village   b) unknown land   c) an island

Clue 3

Johnny went to a *cider mill* to get the apple seeds. He wanted to see thousands of trees growing in apple *orchards* all over the United States. Johnny told the people to eat the apples as soon as they were *harvested*.

6. A *cider mill* is_____ (n).
   a) a place where apples are crushed   b) a place where flour is made
   c) a farm

7. An *orchard* is _____ (n).
   a) a store   b) a farm of fruit trees   c) a garage

8. *Harvest* means _____ (v).
   a) to plant   b) to water   c) to gather

Clue 4

Johnny always walked *barefoot,* but the first time he carried his apple seeds to the pioneers, Johnny took a *canoe* down the Ohio River.

9. *Barefoot* means _____ (adj).
   a) fast   b) without shoes   c) on tiptoe

10. A *canoe* is _____ (n).
    a) a boat   b) a train   c) a wagon

Clue 5

Johnny loved all animals and cried when he killed a *rattlesnake* that had bitten him. Because he was a *vegetarian* he only ate nuts and berries.

11. A *rattlesnake* is _____ (n).
    a) a bird   b) a spider   c) a poisonous snake

12. A *vegetarian* is _____ (n).
    a) a carrot   b) a person who doesn't eat meat   c) an animal doctor

Questions for Discussion

First, reread the story carefully looking for the deeper meanings and reviewing the vocabulary. Then in groups of four discuss the following questions with your classmates. Be sure to tell what your native culture is.
1. What was your favorite sentence in this story and why?
2. Was Johnny Appleseed a hero? Explain.
3. If you met Johnny Appleseed would you respect him or would you think he was crazy?

Putting All the Pieces Together

Look at the puzzles on page 18 and page 23. Find the pieces that fit this story and discuss what cultural values this hero tale teaches American children.

Double-checking the Vocabulary

Fill in the crossword with the following vocabulary words: pioneer, orchards, vast, cider mill, canoe, vegetarian, rattlesnake, eccentric, missionary, wilderness, harvest, barefoot.

Across

1. a person who eats no meat
2. enormous, great in size
3. a poisonous snake that makes a noise of warning
4. one of the first settlers in a new land
5. an area of land with no human presence
6. very strange

Down

7. the act of gathering the crops
8. farms of fruit trees
9. the place where apples are crushed to make a drink from the apple juice
10. a person who teaches and spreads his or her religion to others
11. not wearing shoes
12. a long, light, narrow boat moved by a paddle

Writing

Think, *in English*, about the most similar story in your culture. Then, using the vocabulary words, write it, *in English*, in correct American form and as briefly as possible.

Speaking

Now, tell your story.

The Wonderful Wizard of Oz

Reading Readiness

A. With a partner look at this book cover. Describe what you see. Try to guess the names of the characters in the story and what the story will be about.

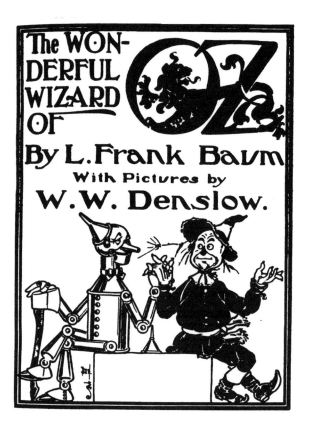

B. Look at these questions and share your ideas with the class.
1. Have you ever wanted something very badly only to discover that you always had it?
2. Can you expect someone to do you a favor if you do nothing in return?

Background Notes

The following is a very short version of a 260 page book published in 1900 by L. Frank Baum. That book is considered the best original American fantasy written before 1900. It is a story about a little girl who meets some very strange new friends in a strange land. They go on a long journey together, and all of them finally find what they are looking for. In 1902, Baum wrote and produced a musical play called *The Wizard of Oz*. Two silent films were made of the story, one in 1910 and one in 1925. In 1939 the movie studio MGM produced a Technicolor version of this tale and *The Wizard of Oz* became the most beloved story in America. You might want to see the video of that marvelous film after you read this story.

Reading Selection

Now read this story once, as quickly as possible, for the general idea. Try to guess the meanings of the words you don't understand by the context. You can underline the words you don't know, but don't stop reading.

Dorothy lived in the midst of the great Kansas prairies with Uncle Henry, who was a farmer, and Aunt Em, his wife. When Dorothy stood in the doorway of their small house everything looked flat and gray and dull. Nothing had any life or joy or sparkle. When Dorothy, who was an orphan, first came to live there, Aunt Em had been startled by the child's laughter and still was filled with wonder that Dorothy could find anything to be merry about. It was Toto that made Dorothy laugh and saved her from growing as gray as her surroundings. Toto was not gray. He was a little black dog who played all day long. Dorothy played with him and loved him dearly.

But today they were not playing because the sky was grayer than usual and Uncle Henry said a cyclone was coming. "Quick, into the storm cellar!" screamed Aunt Em. But Toto ran under the bed, and Dorothy ran to get him. There was a great shriek from the wind, and the house started to shake so hard Dorothy fell on the floor. Then a strange thing happened. The house whirled around and rose slowly in the air like a hot air balloon. Dorothy looked out the window and realized that she, Toto, and the house were being carried high up in the middle of the cyclone. Dorothy was frightened at first, but after many hours she finally lay down on her bed and fell asleep.

She was awakened by a shock so sudden and severe that if she had not been lying on the soft bed she might have been hurt. She noticed that the house was no longer moving and jumped from her bed with

Toto in her arms. Opening the front door, she gave a cry of amazement and saw a country of marvelous beauty and bright colors. A group of very small people came toward her. There were three men and one very old and wrinkled woman, who bowed to Dorothy and said, "You are welcome, most noble sorceress, to the land of the Munchkins. We are grateful to you for having killed the Wicked Witch of the East and for setting our people free from bondage." "You are very kind, but there must be some mistake. I have not killed anything," said Dorothy. "Your house did, anyway," replied the little old woman with a laugh, "and that is the same thing. See!" And she pointed to the bottom of the house. "There are her two feet sticking out." Dorothy gave a little cry of fright. Beneath her house were two feet with silver shoes on them. "There is the Wicked Witch of the East. Now she is dead and the Munchkins are free." "Are you a Munchkin?" asked Dorothy. "No, I am their friend, the Witch of the North, and they sent for me when your house killed the Witch of the East. I am not as powerful as she was, or I should have set the people free myself. Now there are only three witches left in all the Land of Oz, and only one is wicked, the one who lives in the West. Those of the North and South are good witches. Here, take the witch's shoes. There is some charm connected with them." And she put the silver shoes on Dorothy. "Oh, thank you, but I really just want to get back to my aunt and uncle in Kansas. Can you help me find my way?" "Oh, I am sorry, but I cannot help. You must go to the City of Emeralds. Perhaps the Great Oz can help you. He is a good wizard. You must walk there and it is very far. I will give you my kiss and no one will dare injure a person who has been kissed by the Witch of the North." She kissed Dorothy gently on the forehead and her lips left a round shining mark. "The road to the Wizard is paved with yellow brick. You cannot miss it. Good-bye, my dear." And the witch whirled around three times and suddenly disappeared.

Dorothy and Toto started to walk on the road of yellow brick. After several miles they stopped to rest by a cornfield. She saw a scarecrow and was surprised to hear him say, "Good day." "Did you speak?" she asked. "Certainly, and who are you?" the Scarecrow answered. "My name is Dorothy, and I am going to the Emerald City to ask the great Oz to send me back to Kansas." "Where is the Emerald City?" asked the Scarecrow. "You don't know?" asked Dorothy. "No indeed. I don't know anything. You see, I am stuffed, so I have no brains at all. It is an uncomfortable feeling to know one is a fool. Do you think the great Oz would give me some brains?" "I cannot tell, but you may come with me if you like. If Oz will not give you any brains you will be no worse off than you are now."

And so they continued walking on the road of yellow brick. Dorothy told her story, and the Scarecrow said, "I cannot understand why you should wish to leave this beautiful country and go back to the dry, gray place you call Kansas." "That is because you have no brains. No matter how dreary and gray our homes are, we people of flesh and blood would rather live there than any other country, be it ever so beautiful. There is no place like home," said Dorothy.

The next day they entered a dark forest. Suddenly they heard a groaning sound. Toto barked, and Dorothy and the Scarecrow saw a man made entirely of tin. He stood perfectly still, "Please get the oil can. I am all rusted," he said. "I might have stood there always if you had not come by. You have saved my life. But why are you here in the forest?" "We are going to see the Wizard of Oz and ask him to give me a brain," said the Scarecrow. "Do you need something he could give you?" "Oh," said the Tinman, "I will tell you my sad story. You see, I was once a man who was in love with a beautiful Munchkin girl. But her mother asked the Wicked Witch of the East to put a spell on me, and one day as I was chopping wood, my ax chopped off my left leg. A tinsmith made me a leg of tin and this angered the witch, so she made my ax slip again and chop off my right leg. The tinsmith then made me a right leg of tin. The charm caused me to cut off both my arms and then my head. Each time the tinsmith made me parts. Then the wicked witch made my ax cut through my body, and the tinsmith again came to my help. But alas, he didn't put a heart inside my new tin body, and I lost the love I had for that girl. I had a brain once," he said to the Scarecrow "and I don't miss it at all!" "All the same," said the Scarecrow, "I shall ask for brains instead of a heart, for a fool would not know what to do with a heart if he had one." "I shall ask Oz for a heart," said the Tin Woodman, "for brains do not make one happy and happiness is the best thing in the world."

And so they continued on the yellow brick road, which led deeper and deeper into the forest. Suddenly they heard a terrible roar, and a lion jumped into the road. He knocked over the Scarecrow and the Tin Woodman and turned to Toto. Dorothy, fearing Toto would be killed, rushed forward and slapped the Lion on the nose. "Don't you dare bite Toto. You ought to be ashamed of yourself!" And the Lion started to cry.

"Why, you are a coward!" "I know it," said the Lion, wiping a tear from his eye with the tip of his tail. "It is my great sorrow and makes my life very unhappy. But whenever there is danger my heart begins to beat fast." "Why don't you ask the great Oz to give you courage?" "Oh, I will, for as long as I know myself to be a coward I will never be happy."

And so the four friends and Toto continued on the yellow brick road, which led into a beautiful field of scarlet poppies. Now it is well known that when there are so many of those flowers together their odor is so powerful that anyone who breathes it falls deep asleep. And that is what happened to Dorothy, Toto, and the Lion. "Let us carry Dorothy and Toto out or they will die. We can make a chair with our hands," said the Scarecrow. "We must leave the Lion," said the Tin Woodman, crying, "Perhaps he will dream that he has found courage at last." Just then, the Queen of the Field Mice came and offered to have her subjects tie ropes to the Lion and drag him from the poppy field. That done, the Lion, Dorothy, and Toto awakened, and they continued their journey to the Emerald City, which they could see in the distance.

At the gates of the Emerald City there was a big bell, which they rang. A man called the Guardian of the Gate made them put on green glasses, which he locked on their heads with a little lock. When they entered the city everything was completely green, the streets, the houses, the people, even the sky. They were told that they must enter the throne room of the great Oz separately, and Dorothy was to go first. In the large room Dorothy saw a chair, and in the center of the chair was an enormous head without a body to support it. The mouth of the Head moved and said, "I am Oz, the Great and Terrible. Who are you and why do you seek me?"

"I am Dorothy, the Small and Meek. I have come to you for help."

"Where did you get the silver shoes, where did you get the mark on your forehead, and what do you seek from me?" the Head asked. When Dorothy had explained everything, the Head said, "You have no right to expect me to send you back to Kansas unless you do something for me in return. In this country everyone must pay for everything he gets. Help me and I will help you. Kill the Wicked Witch of the West and I will send you back to Kansas."

Dorothy and her friends were terribly disappointed and afraid but there was nothing else they could do. They all so badly wanted what they lacked that they decided to try to find and kill the Witch although it was terribly dangerous. They went toward the West, and the Witch saw them coming. She sent her Winged Monkeys to destroy them. The Monkeys swooped down on the Scarecrow and Tinman, lifted them high in the air, and dropped them, and the Scarecrow and the Tin Woodman fell apart. They tied up the Lion and flew him to the Witch's castle and put him in a cage. But Dorothy they did not harm at all. "We dare not harm this girl," said the leader of the Winged Monkeys, "for she is protected by the Power of Good and that is greater than the Power of Evil. All we can do is to carry her to the castle of the Wicked Witch and leave her there." The Witch made Dorothy her slave because Dorothy did not know her own power. She worked very hard each day for the Witch and visited the poor Lion in his cage and brought him food. What the Witch really wanted were the silver shoes. One day, as Dorothy was mopping the floor, the Witch made Dorothy trip over a bar of invisible iron, and one of the shoes fell off. The Witch grabbed it, and Dorothy got very angry. "Give me back my shoe! It's mine! You have no right to take it!" "I shall keep it and get the other one too!" the Witch laughed. Dorothy was so angry, she grabbed a bucket of water and threw it at the Witch. "See what you have done!" screamed the Witch. "In a minute I shall melt away!" And the Witch actually melted away like sugar.

Dorothy picked up her shoe and went to free the Lion. They were no longer prisoners in a strange land. They asked the Winged Monkeys to fetch the Scarecrow and Tin Woodman. Dorothy and the Lion put their friends back together again and once more set off to the Emerald City. "I shall get to Kansas, and I shall get my brain, and I shall get my heart, and I shall get my courage," the friends all said happily.

As before, the Guardian of the Gate put green glasses on them, and they went to the palace. But the Great Oz made them wait many days. Finally he let them enter the throne room. There was nothing there except a voice that filled the room. "I am Oz, the Great and Terrible. Why do you seek me?" "We have come to claim our promise. The Wicked Witch of the West is destroyed!" As they were talking, Toto knocked down a screen that stood in the corner, and the next moment they saw a little old man with a bald head and a wrinkled face who seemed as surprised as they were. "I am Oz, the Great and Terrible," he said, "and I have been making believe." "Oh! no!" the four friends said in their disappointment. "Then you are nothing but a humbug!" "Yes, I am a ventriloquist and a balloonist who worked for the circus in Omaha, Nebraska. One day I went up in the balloon and the ropes got twisted and I couldn't come down. I floated for a long time and gradually came down here. Of course the people thought I was a great wizard coming from the sky, and I let them think so. I ordered this city to be built and put green glasses on all the people and called it the Emerald City." "Oh, I think you are a very bad man," said Dorothy. "Oh, no, my dear. I'm really a very good man, but I'm a very bad wizard." "Can't you give me brains?" asked the Scarecrow. "You don't need them. You are learning something every day. A baby has brains, but it doesn't know much. Experience is the only thing that brings knowledge, and the longer you are on earth the more experience you are sure to get. But I shall stuff your head with bran and needles." The Wizard did this, and then he said, "Hereafter you will be a great man, for I have given you a lot of bran-new brains. The needles will be proof that you are sharp." And the Scarecrow felt wise indeed.

"How about my heart?" asked the Tin Woodman. "Why I think you are wrong to want a heart. It makes most people unhappy. If you only knew it, you are in luck to not have a heart." "I will bear the unhappiness without a murmur, if you will give me the heart," said the Tinman. So the Wizard opened a drawer and took out a pretty heart made of silk and stuffed with sawdust. He cut a little hole in the Woodman's chest and put the heart in, and the Woodman was very happy.

"What about my courage?" asked the Lion anxiously. "You have plenty of courage, I am sure. All you need is confidence in yourself. There is nothing that is not afraid when it faces danger. True courage is in facing danger when you are afraid, and that kind of courage you have plenty of." Then the Wizard went to the cupboard and took down a green bottle. He poured liquid from the bottle into a dish and said to the Lion, "Drink. If it were inside of you it would be courage. You know of course, courage is always inside one, so drink it quickly." "Oh, I feel so full of courage," said the Lion joyfully.

"And now, how am I to get back to Kansas?" said Dorothy. And the Wizard asked Dorothy to help him make a balloon out of green silk. It took three days, and then Oz told all the people that he had to visit his great brother wizard who lived in the clouds. "While I am gone, the Scarecrow, who is wise, will rule over you." He filled the balloon with hot air, got in the basket, and called for Dorothy, who was looking for Toto. Suddenly, crack, snap, the ropes broke, and up the balloon rose without Dorothy. "Come back!" she screamed. "I want to go, too." "I can't come back, my dear," called Oz from the basket. "Good-bye."

Dorothy wept bitterly because she wanted to get back to Kansas. Then the four friends heard that if they traveled to the land of the Quadlings they could ask Glinda the Good Witch of the South to help Dorothy go home. They traveled very far and had many adventures and were finally at the palace of the beautiful Witch Glinda. "Your silver shoes will carry you to Kansas. If you had known their power you could have gone back to your Aunt Em the very first day you came to this country." "But then we should not have had our brains, heart, and courage," said the three friends. "That is all true. And I am glad I was of use to these good friends. But now that each one has found his happiness I think I should like to go back to Kansas," said Dorothy. "All you have to do is to knock the heels together three times and command the shoes to carry you wherever you wish to go," said Glinda. Dorothy kissed her friends good-bye and, holding Toto in her arms, clapped the heels of her shoes together three times and said, "Take me home to Aunt Em!" Instantly she was whirling though the air and suddenly was sitting on the broad Kansas prairie in front of the new farmhouse Uncle Henry had built after the cyclone had carried away the old one. The silver shoes were gone; they must have fallen off on the way.

Aunt Em had just come out of the house when she saw Dorothy. "My darling child," she said, covering Dorothy's face with kisses. "Where in the world did you come from?" "From the Land of Oz," said Dorothy, "and here is Toto, too. And oh, Aunt Em. I'm so glad to be at home again!"

Checking Your Comprehension

Answer these questions in class.

1. How does Dorothy get the silver shoes?
2. Why is the Emerald City green?
3. How do the three friends get what they are lacking?
4. Why does it take Dorothy such a long time to go home?

Be a Vocabulary Detective

Working in pairs, look for hints and guess the vocabulary from the context clues. Then fill in the blanks with the correct answers.

Clue 1

Dorothy is an *orphan* who lives in Kansas on the flat *prairie.* The land is very gray, but she is so bright that she often *startles* her *wrinkled* aunt and uncle with laughter. Kansas often has terrible *cyclones,* so Uncle Henry has built a *storm cellar* to protect them.

1. An *orphan* is _____ (n).
   a) a sister   b) a mother   c) a parentless child

2. A *prairie* is _____ (n).
   a) flat land   b) farms   c) hills

3. *Startle* means _____ (v).
   a) to surprise   b) to calm   c) to annoy

4. *Wrinkled* means _____ (adj).
   a) smooth   b) young   c) lined

5. A *cyclone* is _____ (n).
   a) a flood   b) an earthquake   c) a windstorm

6. A *storm cellar* is _____ (n).
   a) an attic   b) a garage   c) a room under the ground

Clue 2

The Witch of the North thinks that Dorothy is also some kind of a *sorceress* like she is. After she kisses Dorothy, she *whirls* three times and disappears.

7. A *sorceress* is _____ (n).
   a) a teacher   b) a magician   c) an ogre

8. *Whirl* means _____ (v).
   a) to spin   b) to dance   c) to jump

Clue 3

Oz is really only a circus *ventriloquist,* with a talent for throwing his voice and doing tricks. He is not really a wizard, he is just a *humbug.*

9. A *ventriloquist* is _____ (n).
   a) a witch   b) an entertainer   c) a boxer

10. A *humbug* is _____ (n).
   a) a liar   b) an honest person   c) a dangerous person

Clue 4

The Witch wants to find Dorothy so she has her Monkeys *seek* her. The Witch plans to hold Dorothy in *bondage,* and Dorothy is so afraid of the Witch that she is very *meek* until the Witch steals Dorothy's shoe.

11. *Seek* means_____ (v).
    a) to look   b) to find   c) to lose

12. *Bondage* is _____ (n).
    a) freedom   b) slavery   c) marriage

13. *Meek* means _____ (adj).
    a) strong   b) weak   c) gentle

Questions for Discussion

First, reread the story carefully looking for the deeper meanings and reviewing the vocabulary. Then in groups of four discuss the following questions with your classmates. Be sure to tell what your native culture is.
1. What was your favorite sentence in this story and why?
2. Do you agree that there is no place like home even when it is gray and dull?
3. What did Glinda mean when she said that Dorothy could have gone home earlier, because she had the power all the time?
4. Did you think the following was funny? ". . . for I have given you a lot of bran-new brains. The needles will be proof that you are sharp." Making a joke with words is called a pun. See if you can figure out the joke. (It is very "punny"!)

Putting All the Pieces Together

Look at the puzzles on page 18 and page 23. Find the pieces that fit this story and discuss what cultural values this story teaches American children.

Double-checking the Vocabulary

Look at the definitions and cross out the words in the list that match. Then, looking at the words that remain, read from left to right, top to bottom, and find the answer to the question, What does Dorothy say about the wonderful land of Oz?

a. to cause to jump or be surprised
b. to turn around very, very fast
c. a child whose mother and father are dead
d. a severe windstorm, a tornado, a twister
e. a wide, treeless, grassy plain of land
f. very timid, afraid
g. a magician (female)
h. someone who can make sounds that seem to come from somewhere else
i. to look for
j. a shelter underground for protection during a cyclone
k. a person who pretends to be something he or she is not
l. a line in paper or fabric and especially in the skin of someone old
m. slavery

prairie	cyclone	orphan	startle	there's	storm cellar
whirl	no	wrinkle	sorceress	bondage	place
seek	like	meek	humbug	home	ventriloquist

Writing

Think, *in English*, about the most similar story in your culture. Then, using the vocabulary words, write it, *in English*, in correct American form and as briefly as possible.

Speaking

Now, tell your story.

Part  3

Endings

I start at the beginning, go to the end, and then stop.
—Anthony Burgess

Additional Themes for Writing or Discussion

Now that you've finished these stories, you must have noticed a surprising repetition of similar themes in many of the stories.

In small groups, identify common themes and then compare and contrast them. You can do this in small group discussions, in writing, or in a presentation to the whole class.

Here are a few suggestions to get you started.

Broken Promises

"Rapunzel"
"Rumpelstiltskin"
"The Frog Prince"
"Beauty and the Beast"
"The Pied Piper of Hamelin"
The Wonderful Wizard of Oz
Pinocchio

Loving Fathers

"The Frog Prince"
"Beauty and the Beast"
Pinocchio
Charlotte s Web

Wicked Stepmothers

"Cinderella"
"Snow White"
"Hansel and Gretel"

Parents Who Yearn to Have Children and Who Are
Delighted to Have a Daughter

"Rapunzel"
"Snow White"
"Sleeping Beauty"

Similar Repetitive Rhymes in the Stories:

"Snow White"
"Goldilocks and the Three Bears"

Important Numbers
Three

"Goldilocks and the Three Bears"
"The Three Little Pigs"
"Jack and the Beanstalk"
"Cinderella"
"The Frog Prince"

Seven

"Snow White"
"Sleeping Beauty"

Can you find even more?

Additional Activities

As previously stated, these stories form a foundation of American language and culture and are therefore referred to in everyday adult conversation. Keep your eyes and ears open and try to collect any references to these stories from newspaper cartoons, television and radio advertisements, billboards, songs, conversations, advice columns, etc. You'll be surprised at how many you can collect in just one week. You could have a contest and see who can collect the most. Try it. You'll like it. You might even live happily ever after!

Bibliography for Future Reading

A good book is the best of friends, the same today and forever.
—Martin Farquhar Tupper, 1810-89

I cannot live without books.
—Thomas Jefferson, Letter to John Adams (June 10, 1815)

Now that you have read some of the most famous stories in the United States, I hope that you are eager to continue to read more and more. By now you should understand how important and enjoyable it is to read the same stories the majority of Americans have read.

The more you read, the larger your vocabulary will grow, and the more you will understand American culture. Each new book will give you another opportunity to share the same reading experiences that Americans have also had.

I recommend that you go to your neighborhood library (it's free!) and ask the librarian to help you choose some books. You can often find both children's and adults' books for 10 cents to 25 cents at garage sales, yard sales, and thrift stores. You can always buy books at some grocery stores and, of course, at bookstores.

The following lists recommend books that have been read by many Americans, both as children and as adults. A number of these books have also become movies or television plays. It was hard to choose which books to put on these lists—there are so many wonderful ones to select from! The following books were chosen because they are so well known, because they are fairly easy for nonnative adults to understand, and because my students liked them the best.

Classic Children's Books

Don't forget to continue reading more stories by the authors in this book. Read the fairy tales of Hans Christian Anderson, the Brothers Grimm, and Charles Perrault, and also read the complete versions of the books that have been abridged or excerpted here—*The Adventures of Pinocchio*, by C. Collodi; *Charlotte's Web*, by E. B. White (as well as his two other books—*Stuart Little* and *The Trumpet of the Swan*); and *The Wonderful Wizard of Oz*, by F. L. Baum.

The following books are classics for little children and are often read aloud to them before they go to sleep. These books are listed in order of difficulty from the easiest to the most difficult, and also in order of length. (They have all been made into cartoons, movies, or musicals. Check your video store after you read them.)

The Cat in the Hat, Horton Hatches the Egg, Green Eggs and Ham (and any of the other books by Dr. Seuss). These are very charming short books in rhyme that will help you with vocabulary and pronunciation.

Madeline, Madeline's Rescue, and *Madeline and the Bad Hat*, by Ludwig Bemelmans. Stories in rhyme about a very strong-willed little girl who lives in a boarding school in Paris.

The Story of Ferdinand by Munro Leaf. A story about individualism and nonconformity and an understanding mother.

The Little Engine That Could, by Watty Piper. An American classic about the importance of believing that you *can* do something.

The Story of Babar, by Jean de Brunhoff. A French children's story about an elephant.

Winnie-the-Pooh, by A. A. Milne. A British tale about a little boy, Christopher Robin, and his adventures with his stuffed animal friends, a bear (Pooh), a donkey, a pig, and a tiger.

Mary Poppins, by P. L. Travers. A British story of fun and wonder about what happens when a magical woman comes to take care of four children.

Peter Pan, by J. M. Barrie. A British fantasy about a little boy who doesn't want to grow up and his adventures in Never-Never Land.

Alice in Wonderland and *Through the Looking Glass* by Lewis Carroll. The adventures of a little girl in a new, strange world.

Middle School Level Books

The following is a list of books read by children in elementary and junior high schools. The books are listed by subject and from the easiest to the most difficult.

The following are books about American history.

Little House on the Prairie (and all the "Little House" books), by Laura Ingalls Wilder. A true story written by Laura herself (autobiography) of Laura Ingalls and her family as Laura grows up on the prairies of America in the 1890s. These books will really help you understand American values.

Caddie Woodlawn, by Carol Ryrie Brink. The true story (biography) of Brink's grandmother, who grew up on the American frontier. A lot of very funny incidents occur in this book.

The Light in the Forest, by Conrad Richter. The true story of what happened to a four year old American boy who was raised by Native Americans and then returned "home" when he was grown.

The Witch of Blackbird Pond, by Elizabeth George Speare. A girl grows up in the East in the 1800s and makes friends with an old woman.

Island of the Blue Dolphins, by Scott O'Dell. The true story of a Native American girl who spends eighteen years living alone on an island near Catalina.

Sarah, Plain and Tall, by Patricia MacLachlan. Sarah answers a widower's ad for a wife, and his two children hope that their father will marry her. Caution: It may make you cry.

My Brother Sam Is Dead, by James Lincoln Collier and Christopher Collier. A historical novel of the Revolutionary War.

The following books are stories about animals.

Where the Red Fern Grows, by Wilson Rawls. The love between a boy and his dog.

The Red Pony, by John Steinbeck. A sad, beautiful story about a boy and his horse.

Black Beauty, by Anna Sewell; A beautiful black horse is sold and has many adventures.

Here is another book that you might enjoy reading.

Heidi, by Johanna Spyri. The story of a young girl who grows up in the mountains of Switzerland.

Teenage Level Books

The following is a list of books read by American teenagers.

The Diary of a Young Girl, by Anne Frank. The true story of a young girl living during the Holocaust in Holland. She died in a German concentration camp. Her father survived and later found her diary, which he published. This book has been translated into many languages.

Anastasia Krupnik (and any other novel), by Lois Lowry. Becoming a teenager in modern America.

Onion John, by Joseph Krumgold. A friendship between a twelve year old boy and an immigrant handyman.

And Now Miguel, by Joseph Krumgold. A twelve year old wants to go with his relatives to herd sheep. A story of Mexican Americans and growing up.

Dicey's Song (and any other novel), by Cynthia Voigt. The sad story of four children abandoned by their mother and their long walk in search of their grandmother.

Mom, the Wolf Man, and Me (and any other novel), by Norma Klein. A teenage favorite about a single mother, her son, and her male friends.

Summer of My German Soldier, by Bette Green. A young Jewish girl makes friends with a German prisoner of war in Arkansas during World War II.

Killing Mr. Griffin (and any other novel), by Lois Duncan. Students plan to scare their teacher, but he dies of a heart attack. What should they do?

Adult Level Books

The following is a list of famous books read by American adults. They are listed from the easiest to the most difficult.

The Little Prince, by Antoine Saint-Exupéry. Translated from the French, this beautiful story about the complicated ideas of friendship and love is told in simple language. You might have read this book in your own language; now read it in English!

The Pearl, by John Steinbeck. This story is set in Mexico. A poor fisherman finds a valuable pearl and learns, with sadness, that love is more valuable than money.

The Old Man and the Sea, by Ernest Hemingway. A classic of American literature about old age, self-esteem and succeeding against difficulties.

Shane, by Jack Schaefer. A classic cowboy story.

The House on Mango Street, by Sandra Cisneros. Short stories about growing up in a Mexican-American community.

Thousand Pieces of Gold, by Ruthanne Lum McCunn. The biography of Lalu Nathoy, born in China in 1853, who was kidnaped as a slave and sent to America in 1872. She died an American citizen in 1933.

Farewell to Manzanar, by Jeanne Wakatsuki Houston. The true story of the 100,000 Japanese-Americans kept as prisoners of war in the United States during World War II. An autobiography.

Nectar in a Sieve, by Kamala Markandaya. The beautiful story of a girl in India from her marriage at twelve until the death of her husband thirty years later. A story of poverty and the strength of love.

China Men, by Maxine Hong Kingston. A fascinating history of the Chinese-Americans in the United States told as part of the author's autobiography.